THE PENGUIN PO

# THE NEW POE



A. Alvarez was born in London in 1929 and educated at Oundle School and Corpus Christi College, Oxford. For a time he researched and taught in Oxford and America, but since 1956 has lived as a freelance writer in London, travelling a good deal and making occasional academic forays to the States – including a trip as Visiting Professor of English at the State University of New York at Buffalo. He delivered the Gauss Seminars on criticism at Princeton University in 1958.

A. Alvarez was the Advisory Editor of the Penguin Modern European Poets series while it was in existence. He has been poetry editor and critic for the *Observer*, a contributor to the *New Statesman* for ten years and its drama critic from 1958 to 1960. In 1961 he received the Vachel Lindsay Prize for Poetry from *Poetry* (Chicago). His other publications include *The Shaping Spirit*, *The School of Donne*, *Under Pressure*, *Beyond All This Fiddle*, *The Savage God*, *Hers*, *Hunt*, *Life After Marriage* and *The Biggest Game in Town*. He has written several volumes of poetry, including No 18 of *Penguin Modern Poets* and *Autumn to Autumn*.

# THE NEW POETRY

AN ANTHOLOGY SELECTED AND INTRODUCED BY

A. ALVAREZ

PENGUIN BOOKS

PENGUIN BOOKS

Published by the Penguin Group
27 Wrights Lane, London W8 5TZ, England
Viking Penguin Inc., 40 West 23rd Street, New York, New York 10010, USA
Penguin Books Australia Ltd, Ringwood, Victoria, Australia
Penguin Books Canada Ltd, 2801 John Street, Markham, Ontario, Canada L3R 1B4
Penguin Books (NZ) Ltd, 182–190 Wairau Road, Auckland 10, New Zealand

Penguin Books Ltd, Registered Offices: Harmondsworth, Middlesex, England

This selection first published 1962
Reprinted 1964
Revised Edition 1966
Reprinted 1967, 1968, 1969, 1970, 1971, 1972, 1973, 1974, 1976,
1978, 1980, 1982, 1984, 1986, 1988



Set, printed and bound in Great Britain by
Cox & Wyman Ltd, Reading
Set in Monotype Bembo

TO MY SON

ADAM

## CONTENTS

Prefatory Note 17
Preface to the Revised Edition 17
Acknowledgements 19
Introduction: The New Poetry, *or* Beyond the Gentility Principle 21

## THE AMERICANS

JOHN BERRYMAN (1917–72). Born in Oklahoma, educated at Columbia and Cambridge, taught at Harvard and Princeton before becoming a Professor at the University of Minnesota, where he died. His books include *The Dispossessed* (1948), *Homage to Mistress Bradstreet* (1953), two volumes of *Dream Songs* (1964 and 1968), a novel, *Recovery*, and a study of Stephen Crane. His *Selected Poems* were published in England in 1972.

The Statue 33
The Moon and the Night and the Men 35
The Ball Poem 36
The Song of the Tortured Girl 37
Whether there is Sorrow in the Demons 37
New Year's Eve 38
*from* Homage to Mistress Bradstreet 41

ROBERT LOWELL (1917–77). Born in Boston, educated at Harvard and Kenyon. He lived and worked mostly in New York, moving to England for a period in the 1970s. His books include *Land of Unlikeness* (1944), *Lord Weary's Castle* (1946), *Poems 1938–49* (1950), *Life Studies* (1959), *Imitations* (1962), *For the Union Dead* (1965), *Notebooks* (1970) and several plays. His last book, *Day by Day*, was published just after his death in New York in 1977.

The Quaker Graveyard in Nantucket 43
France 47
Mr Edwards and the Spider 48
Waking in the Blue 49
Man and Wife 51
'To Speak of the Woe that is in Marriage' 52
Skunk Hour 52

D. J. ENRIGHT (*b.* 1920) is at present Professor of English in the University of Malaya, Singapore. Publications include three books of verse, three novels, a book on Japan, and a collection of literary criticism.



DONALD DAVIE (*b.* 1922) has lived and taught in Dublin (from 1950 to 1957) and, since 1958, in Cambridge. As well as collections of poetry, he has published two books of literary criticism.



PHILIP LARKIN (*b.* 1922) has written a novel, *A Girl in Winter*, and two books of poetry.

CONTENTS

CONTENTS

JOHN WAIN (*b.* 1925) was Lecturer in English at Reading University before resigning to devote more time to his writing. This covers novels, critical essays, poetry and journalism.

The Bad Thing 123
Poem 123
The New Sun 125
Poem Without a Main Verb 126
Au Jardin des Plantes 127

ARTHUR BOYARS (*b.* 1925) has published poetry and criticism in many magazines and reviews, and edited *Mandrake* from 1946 until 1957. He is currently editing *The International Literary Annual*.

Lovers in a Park 128
Horses 129
Initial 130
Final Day 133
Florence: Garibaldi Day 1949 133

CHRISTOPHER MIDDLETON (*b.* 1926) is Lecturer in German at London University. He has written articles, broadcast, and published translations of modern German poetry. His first poems appeared in 1944, and a further collection (*Torse* 3) is due.

At Porthcothan 135
Aesthetics for Benetto Gulgo 137
Alba after Six Years 138
Edward Lear in February 138
The Thousand Things 139

CHARLES TOMLINSON (*b.* 1927) has lived in Italy and London and now teaches at Bristol University. His first volume of poems was originally published in the U.S.A.

Winter Encounters 140
How Still the Hawk 141
Poem 141
Farewell to Van Gogh 142
The Churchyard Wall 142

CONTENTS

CONTENTS

TED HUGHES (*b.* 1930) is a Yorkshireman. His books of poetry, *The Hawk in the Rain* and *Lupercal*, have won awards in Britain and America.

Famous Poet 172
Wind 173
October Dawn 174
Vampire 175
February 176
A Woman Unconscious 177
Esther's Tomcat 178
Hawk Roosting 179
To Paint a Water Lily 180
The Bull Moses 181
View of a Pig 182
An Otter 183
Thrushes 185
Pike 186
Snowdrop 187
Sunstroke 188
Gog 189
Pibroch 190

JON SILKIN (*b.* 1930) has worked as a manual labourer and taught English to foreign students as well as publishing several books of poetry, including *The Peaceable Kingdom* and *Nature with Man*. He also edits with Ken Smith the literary periodical *Quarterly Stand* which he started in 1952.

Death of a Son 191
The Child 192
Lilies of the Valley 195
A Daisy 196
Dandelion 197

GEOFFREY HILL (*b.* 1932) was educated at Oxford. *For the Unfallen*, his first volume of poetry, was published in 1959.

Genesis 198
God's Little Mountain 200
Holy Thursday 200

Easter Poem 225
Porpoises 226

DAVID WEVILL (*b.* 1935) comes from Canada. He read history and English at Cambridge and has lived in England ever since, apart from two years when he taught English at Mandalay University. His first collection of poems, *Birth of a Shark*, appeared in 1964.

Spiders 228
Separation 229
The Birth of a Shark 230
Street Stroller 233
The Crèche 233

JOHN FULLER (*b.* 1937) is doing research at New College, Oxford, where he won the Newdigate Prize in 1960. He has published *Fairground Music*, a collection of his poems.

White Queen 235
Band Music 235
Mercury 236
Owls 236
Green Fingers 237

IAN HAMILTON (*b.* 1938) is editor of *The Review*. He received the E. C. Gregory Award in 1963 and published a pamphlet-collection of poems, *Pretending Not to Sleep*, in 1964.

The Storm 238
The Recruits 238
Trucks 239
Last Illness 239
Pretending not to Sleep 240

Index of First Lines 241
Index of Poets 247

## PREFATORY NOTE

This is a personal anthology. It makes no claims to give a sample of every kind of verse now being written in Great Britain. A number of more or less well-known names have been left out – though none, I hope, by oversight. I am, however, trying to represent what I think is the most significant work of the British poets who began to come into their own in the fifties. I have also included the work of two American writers who, although established before then, seem, as I try to explain in the Introduction, to be concerned with problems that some of the new generation of poets over here are beginning to face. Otherwise, I have, often regretfully, not included new work by poets whose reputations were made before 1950 – Auden, MacNeice, Graves, MacDiarmid, Henry Reed, Patrick Kavanagh – nor that of young writers, like Peter Porter and Sylvia Plath, who, although living in this country, are not British. I have further limited the selection by including never fewer than five poems by any one poet.

This is not, in short, an anthology for the reader who wants a complete guide to the contemporary poetic scene; but then, anyone who wants that already has a large number of excellent collections from which to choose. In this book I am, instead, simply attempting to give my idea of what, that really matters, has happened to poetry in England during the last decade.

A.A. 1962

## PREFACE TO THE REVISED EDITION

When *The New Poetry* first appeared a number of reviewers commented on the discrepancy between the generally rather sober verse and the inflammatory introduction. Certainly, the gap was there and perhaps inevitable. The anthology was a collection of the poems I most liked from the period, whilst the introduction was, at least in part, an attempt to read the entrails and prophesy the direction poetry might soon take.

To some extent, I seem to have been proved right. This is not simply a question of the ideas in the introduction being taken up by one group or another and handed out again in oddly changed forms. That did happen, but it was merely a phenomenon of literary fashion-mongering – not in itself particularly meaningful. What is more important is that the essay seemed to correspond to some genuine poetic reality and even hit a responsive nerve in one or two serious writers. So perhaps it helped clear the ground a little for work which was beginning to be done.

Some of the self-imposed restrictions of the first edition no longer seem necessary or justified, particularly the decision to include, apart from Lowell and Berryman, only British poets. Inexplicably, neither Sylvia Plath nor Anne Sexton were represented in the Penguin anthology of contemporary American verse. That in itself would have been reason enough to print them here, if it were not also that their work, more than anyone else's, makes sense of my introduction. Ideally, I would have wished to include far more of Sylvia Plath's poems but her literary executors felt, reasonably enough, that this might interfere with the sale of her first posthumous collection, *Ariel.* So I have taken only four poems from that book, plus another three from the mass of her verse that is still to be published. Peter Porter, an Australian, and David Wevill, a Canadian, are now settled in England, so it would be unnecessarily pernickety to leave them out, as well as a loss to the anthology. I have added work by four Englishmen, most of whose best verse seems to me to have been written since this anthology first appeared. Three poems by Ted Hughes have been removed at his request; otherwise the only one of the original contributors whose poems are other than those in the first edition is John Fuller who, because of a mutual misunderstanding, was inadequately represented.

1965 A. ALVAREZ

# ACKNOWLEDGEMENTS

The Introduction has been published, with slight alterations, in *Commentary*. An extremely abbreviated version of it appeared in the 'In Our Time' series in the *Observer*. I am grateful to the editors of both journals for their permission to reprint the piece.

For permission to publish or reproduce the poems in this anthology, acknowledgement is made to the following:

For John Berryman to Faber & Faber Ltd; for Robert Lowell to Faber & Faber Ltd; for Anne Sexton to Oxford University Press; for Sylvia Plath to Ted Hughes and *Encounter*; for Norman MacCaig to Hogarth Press and the author; for R. S. Thomas to Rupert Hart-Davis Ltd; for D. J. Enright to Hogarth Press, Routledge and Kegan Paul Ltd, and the author; for Donald Davie to Routledge and Kegan Paul Ltd and Marvell Press; for Philip Larkin to Marvell Press and the author; for Kingsley Amis to Victor Gollancz Ltd; for David Holbrook to George Putnam Ltd; for Michael Hamburger to Routledge and Kegan Paul Ltd and the author; for John Wain to Routledge and Kegan Paul Ltd and Macmillan and Co Ltd. for Arthur Boyars to the author; for Christopher Middleton to the author; for Charles Tomlinson to Oxford University Press and Ivan Obolensky Inc.; for Iain Crichton Smith to Eyre & Spottiswoode Ltd; for Thom Gunn to Faber & Faber Ltd and the author; for Peter Porter to Scorpion Press; for Ted Hughes to Faber & Faber Ltd and the author; for Jon Silkin to Chatto and Windus Ltd and Northern House Pamphlets; for Geoffrey Hill to André Deutsch; for George Macbeth to Scorpion Press and the author; for Peter Redgrove to Routledge and Kegan Paul Ltd; for Ted Walker to Jonathan Cape Ltd and the *New Yorker*; for David Wevill to Macmillan and Co. Ltd and the author; for John Fuller to Chatto and Windus Ltd and the author; and for Ian Hamilton to the author.

# THE NEW POETRY
## OR
## BEYOND THE GENTILITY PRINCIPLE

IN 1932 F. R. Leavis proclaimed that Eliot and Pound had between them brought about a significant reorientation of literature. Twenty years later he took most of it back again, blaming the anti-critical workings of the London literary circuit and the decay of an educated reading public. He may have been perfectly justified in crediting the metropolitan pundits with setting up so many false gods. But the relative failure of talent is another matter entirely. So is the manner in which so much of the talent that has arrived has been misused. The London old-boy circuit may often be stupid, conceited, and parasitic but I don't believe that it is in a deliberate conspiracy against good work.

I once suggested (in *The Shaping Spirit*, 1958) that the experimental techniques of Eliot and the rest never really took on in England because they were an essentially American concern: attempts to forge a distinctively American language for poetry. Certainly, since Eliot removed himself into another, remote sphere of influence by proclaiming himself 'Anglo-Catholic in religion, royalist in politics and classicist in literature', the whole movement of English verse has been to correct the balance experimentation had so unpredictably disturbed. Sometime in the twenties Thomas Hardy remarked to Robert Graves that '*vers libre* could come to nothing in England. "All we can do is to write on the old themes in the old styles, but try to do a little better than those who went before us."' Since about 1930 the machinery of modern English poetry seems to have been controlled by a series of negative feed-backs designed to produce precisely the effect Hardy wanted.

The final justification of experimentalism lay, of course, beyond mere technique. The great moderns experimented not just to make it new formally, but to open poetry up to new areas of experience. The kind of insights which had already been substantiated by the novelists – by Melville, Dostoyevsky, Lawrence and even, at times, by Hardy himself – seemed about due to appear in poetry. The negative feed-backs came into action to stop this happening.

The literary historians perhaps would see the process differently. And the English scene is peculiarly amenable to literary history: it is savage with gang-warfare which, at a distance, can be dignified as disagreements between schools of verse. So maybe a little potted, though rather partial, literary history would be in place.

The thirties poets reacted against those of the twenties by asserting that they had no time to be difficult or inward or experimental; the political situation was too urgent. Auden gave them the go-ahead because he combined an extraordinary technical skill in traditional forms with an extraordinary feel for the most contemporary of contemporary idiom. When he began it must really have looked as though he were about to do something quite new in English. In a poem like 'Sir, No Man's Enemy', for example, he used the new, difficult language of psychology with a concentration that was almost Shakespearian; or even in an unambitious piece like 'Lurcher-loving collier, black as night' he managed triumphantly to re-create a traditional lyric – its ancestor is 'Mistress mine, where art thou roaming' – in terms of the contemporary, unromantic, industrial scene. His trouble was that he was too skilful; he found both the art of verse and the art of success too easy. So he was able to channel his deep neurotic disturbances into light verse – much of it, admittedly, very fine – while his contemporary knowingness, his skill with references, with slang, with the time's immediate worries went into the production of a kind of social, occasional verse, mostly traditional in form, but highly up-to-date in idiom. His example encouraged a whole swarm of poetasters who believed, apparently, that to be modern was merely a matter of sounding modern; it had precious little to do with originality. (I would exclude from this Louis MacNeice, whose social-political verse was mostly more effective and certainly more deeply felt than Auden's own.) By the end of the thirties experimental verse was out and traditional forms, in a chic contemporary guise, were back in. That was the first negative feed-back.

The reaction to Auden took the form of anti-intellectualism. He was thought to be too clever and not sufficiently emotional for the extreme circumstances of the forties. The war brought with it a taste for high, if obscure, rhetoric. The log-rolling thirties were followed by the drum-rolling forties. The new master, of course, was Dylan Thomas. But Thomas was not only a fine rhetorician, he also, in his early poems, had something rather original to say. Admittedly, he was under constant pressure from the literary Public Relations Officers to continue at all costs less with his poetry than with his act as the blindly inspired poet; which meant that his rhetoric eventually ran on when the reasons for it had faltered. But the talent was there, however self-destructive it eventually became. His followers, however, used his work as an excuse to kiss *all* meaning good-bye. All that mattered was that the verse should sound impressive. This was the second negative feed-back; a blockage against intelligence.

The third stage was yet another reaction: against wild, loose emotion. The name of the reaction was the Movement, and its anthology was Robert Conquest's *New Lines*. Of the nine poets to appear in this, six, at the time, were university teachers, two librarians, and one a Civil Servant. It was, in short, academic-administrative verse, polite, knowledgeable, efficient, polished, and, in its quiet way, even intelligent. What it had to offer positively was more difficult to describe. Even the editor found he could define it only in negatives: 'It submits to no great systems of theoretical constructs nor agglomerations of unconscious commands. It is free from both mystical and logical compulsions and – like the modern philosophy – is empirical in attitude to all that comes . . . On the more technical side . . . we see the refusal to abandon a rational structure and comprehensible language . . . It will be seen at once that these poets do not have as much in common as they would if they were a group of doctrine-saddled writers forming a definite school complete with programme and rules. What they do have in common is, perhaps, at its lowest, little more than a negative determination to avoid bad principles.'

Mr Conquest is, I think, exaggerating when he says that his poets have nothing very much in common. For example:

> Picture of lover or friend that is not either
> Like you or me who, to sustain our pose,
> Need wine and conversation, colour and light;
> In short, a past that no one now can share,
> No matter whose your future; calm and dry,
> In sex I do not dither more than either,
> Nor should I now swell to halloo the names
> Of feelings that no one needs to remember:
> The same few dismal properties, the same
> Oppressive air of justified unease
> Of our imaginations and our beds.
> It seems the poet made a bad mistake.

Perhaps the logic seems a little tenuous? The shifts a little hard to follow? The content a little too fine-drawn? They should do. The piece is synthetic; it contains eight of the nine *New Lines* poets. I have omitted D. J. Enright since he rarely sticks to the metrical norms on which the rest insist. Otherwise I have not cheated in compiling the poem. I have taken the poets in the order in which they appear in the anthology, without using more than two lines from any one and without changing the punctuation except, in a minor way, between quotations. Yet though the poem may not be quite comprehensible, it is, I think, unified in tone. Wouldn't the impartial reader be hard put to know where one quotation ended and another began? Wouldn't he find a considerable similarity in the quality both of the language and of the experience? A kind of unity of flatness? The pieties of the Movement were as predictable as the politics of the thirties' poets. They are summed up at the beginning of Philip Larkin's 'Church-going':

> Hatless, I take off
> My cycle-clips in awkward reverence.

This, in concentrated form, is the image of the post-war Welfare State Englishman: shabby and not concerned with his appearance; poor – he has a bike, not a car; gauche but full of agnostic piety; underfed, underpaid, overtaxed, hopeless, bored, wry. This is the third negative feed-back: an attempt to show that the poet is not a strange creature inspired; on the contrary, he is just like the man next door – in fact, he probably *is* the man next door.

Now, I am wholly in favour of restoring poetry to the realm of common sense. But there is always the delicate question of how common common sense should be. All three negative feed-backs work, in their different ways, to preserve the idea that life in England goes on much as it always has, give or take a few minor changes in the class system. The upper-middle class, or Tory, ideal – presented in its pure crystalline form by John Betjeman – may have given way to the predominantly lower-middle class, or Labour, ideal of the Movement and the Angries, but the concept of gentility still reigns supreme. And gentility is a belief that life is always more or less orderly, people always more or less polite, their emotions and habits more or less decent and more or less controllable; that God, in short, is more or less good.

It is a stance which is becoming increasingly precarious to maintain. That the English have succeeded so long owes a good deal to the fact that England is an island; it is, literally, insulated from the rest of the world. But since the First World War, that insulation has slowly broken down. Robert Graves's *Goodbye to All That*, for example, shows perfectly how powerless the orthodox defences ultimately became under extreme conditions. When the level of misery was normal the defences worked efficiently enough. His childhood at preparatory and public school meant loneliness, philistinism, lewdness, insensitivity and unhappiness. These were all to be expected, and Graves duly countered them in the orthodox ways: games, toughness, asexual love, wit, and a clipped, dry, you-can't-touch-me manner. He developed, in short, a stiff upper lip. This got him through the first two years of the war, then gradually it broke. The horror of the trenches was too great. What he saw and what he went through was beyond the bounds of anything his training had prepared him for. Physically he survived, but emotionally he could no longer properly cope. The result was a kind of shell-shock which, he says himself, stayed with him for ten years. And even then he had to exile himself from England and erect the elaborate barricade of White Goddesses and classicizing through which his genuine poetry has only slowly and painfully filtered.

In the same way, George Orwell felt he had to purge himself of his governing-class upbringing by deliberately plunging into the abjectest poverty and pain partly, at least, because what he saw in Burma gave the lie to the whole ethos in which he had been raised.

The only English writer who was able to face the more uncompromising forces at work in our time was D. H. Lawrence. And he was born in the working-class and spent most of his life outside England; so he had almost nothing to do with middle-class gentility. 'In those days', he wrote, 'they were always telling me I had genius as though to console me for not having their own incomparable advantages.'

But these forces I have invoked are beyond mere shell-shock and class guilt. They are general and concern us all. What, I suggest, has happened in the last half century is that we are gradually being made to realize that all our lives, even those of the most genteel and enislanded, are influenced profoundly by forces which have nothing to do with gentility, decency or politeness. Theologians would call these forces evil, psychologists, perhaps, libido. Either way, they are the forces of disintegration which destroy the old standards of civilization. Their public faces are those of two world wars, of the concentration camps, of genocide, and the threat of nuclear war.

I do not wish to over-dramatize the situation. War and cruelty have always existed, but those of the twentieth century are different in two ways. First, mass evil (for lack of a better term) has been magnified to match the scale of mass society. We no longer have local wars, we have world wars, which involve the civilians quite as deeply as the military. Where once, at worst, regiments of professional soldiers were wiped out, now whole cities go. Instead of the death of individuals, we have a mass extermination. Instead of individual torture and sadism, we have concentration camps run scientifically as death factories. The disintegration, to put it most mildly, has reached proportions which make it increasingly difficult to ignore. Once upon a time, the English could safely believe that Evil was something that happened on the Continent, or farther off, in the Empire where soldiers were paid to take care of it. To believe this now requires at best an extraordinary single-mindedness, at worst stupidity.

The second, and specifically modern difference in our attitude to the problem is this: the forceable recognition of a mass evil outside us has developed precisely parallel with psychoanalysis; that is, with our recognition of the ways in which the same forces are at work within us. One of the therapeutic purposes, for example, of Bruno Bettelheim's secret psychoanalytic observations when he was in Dachau and Buchenwald was to educate himself into realizing how much of what went on around him expressed what went on inside himself. Another analyst has suggested that the guilt which seems to dog the refugees who escaped from Germany may in part be due to the fact that the Nazis fulfilled the deepest and most primitive drives of the refugees themselves, killing fathers, mothers, brothers, sisters and children. Be this as it may, it is hard to live in an age of psychoanalysis and feel oneself wholly detached from the dominant public savagery. In this way, at least, the makers of horror films are more in tune with contemporary anxiety than most of the English poets.

But as England was not affected by the concentration camps, so it has remained, on the whole, contemptuously impervious to psychology. Primitivism is only generally acknowledged in this country when it takes a peculiarly British form: the domestic sex murder. Then the gloating is public and universal. Had Freud been born in London instead of Vienna, he would probably have finished not in psychoanalysis but in criminology.

I am not suggesting that modern English poetry, to be really modern, must be concerned with psychoanalysis or with the concentration camps or with the hydrogen bomb or with any other of the modern horrors. I am not suggesting, in fact, that it *must* be anything. For poetry that feels it has to cope with pre-determined subjects ceases to be poetry and becomes propaganda. I am, however, suggesting that it drop the pretence that life, give or take a few social distinctions, is the same as ever, that gentility, decency and all the other social totems will eventually muddle through.

What poetry needs, in brief, is a new seriousness. I would define this seriousness simply as the poet's ability and willingness to face the full range of his experience with his full intelligence; not to take the easy exits of either the conventional response or choking incoherence. Believe in it or not, psychology has left its mark on poetry. First, the writer can no longer deny with any assurance the fears and desires he does not wish to face; he knows obscurely that they are there, however skilfully he manages to elude them. Second, having acknowledged their existence, he is no longer absolved from the need to use all his intelligence and skill to make poetic sense of them. Since Freud, the late Romantic dichotomy between emotion and intelligence has become totally meaningless.

This position had, I think, already been partially assumed by T. S. Eliot when he wrote *The Waste Land*. The poem follows, with great precision and delicacy, the movement of a psyche, not just of a society, in the process of disintegration. Eliot's talk of classicism, like his use in the poem of literature and theology, was an elaborate and successful defence which forced impersonality on a deeply personal and painful subject. But during the later twenties and thirties in America, Eliot's technical achievements and the radical revaluation of literary tradition that went with them seemed so bewilderingly impressive that the urgently personal uses this technique was put to were overlooked. A whole school of criticism was developed to prove technically that there was no necessary or even significant connexion between art and its roots in the artist's life. During the forties, however, when English poetry was at its nadir, there arose in the States a new generation of poets, the most important of whom were Robert Lowell and John Berryman. They had assimilated the lesson of Eliot and the critical thirties: they assumed that a poet, to earn his title, had to be very skilful, very original, and very intelligent. But they were no longer concerned with Eliot's rearguard action against the late Romantics; they were, I mean, no longer adherents of the cult of rigid impersonality. So they were able to write poetry of immense

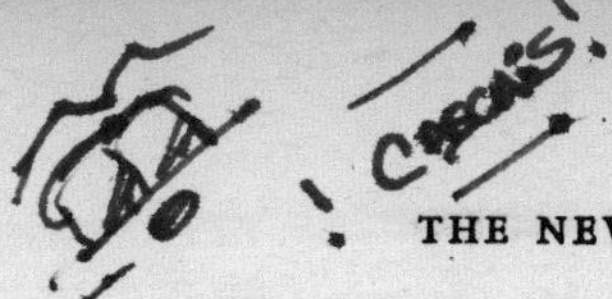



skill and intelligence which coped openly with the quick of their experience, experience sometimes on the edge of disintegration and breakdown. Robert Lowell's latest book, *Life Studies*, for example, is a large step forward in this new direction. It may contain no single poem as impressive as the 'Quaker Graveyard in Nantucket', but the total impact of the book as a whole is altogether more powerful. Where once Lowell tried to externalize his disturbances theologically in Catholicism and rhetorically in certain mannerisms of language and rhythm, he is now, I think, trying to cope with them nakedly, and without evasion.

But to walk naked is, of course, no guarantee of achievement in the arts – often the contrary. Several pieces in *Life Studies* fail for appearing more compulsively concerned with the processes of psychoanalysis than with those of poetry. Conversely, with their deliberate common sense and understatement, some of the Movement poets command, at their best, a self-contained strength and a concern for the discipline of verse which is vital if the art is to remain public. The question is the kind of success a style allows. Compare, for instance, Philip Larkin's 'At Grass' with Ted Hughes's 'A Dream of Horses':

### *At Grass*

The eye can hardly pick them out
From the cold shade they shelter in,
Till wind distresses tail and mane;
Then one crops grass, and moves about
– The other seeming to look on –
And stands anonymous again.

Yet fifteen years ago, perhaps
Two dozen distances sufficed
To fable them: faint afternoons
Of Cups and Stakes and Handicaps,
Whereby their names were artificed
To inlay faded, classic Junes –

Silks at the start: against the sky
Numbers and parasols: outside,
Squadrons of empty cars, and heat,
And littered grass: then the long cry
Hanging unhushed till it subside
To stop-press columns on the street.

Do memories plague their ears like flies?
They shake their heads. Dusk brims the shadows.
Summer by summer, all stole away,
The starting-gates, the crowds and cries –
All but the unmolesting meadows.
Almanacked, their names live; they

Have slipped their names, and stand at ease,
Or gallop for what must be joy,
And not a fieldglass sees them home,
Or curious stop-watch prophesies:
Only the groom, and the groom's boy,
With bridles in the evening come.

Larkin's poem, elegant and unpretentious and rather beautiful in its gentle way, is a nostalgic re-creation of the Platonic (or *New Yorker*) idea of the English scene, part pastoral, part sporting. His horses are *social* creatures of fashionable race meetings and high style; emotionally, they belong to the world of the R.S.P.C.A. It is more skilful but less urgent than 'A Dream of Horses':

We were born grooms, in stable-straw we sleep still,
All our wealth horse-dung and the combings of horses,
And all we can talk about is what horses ail.

Out of the night that gulfed beyond the palace-gate
There shook hooves and hooves and hooves of horses:
Our horses battered their stalls; their eyes jerked white.

And we ran out, mice in our pockets and straw in our hair,
Into darkness that was avalanching to horses
And a quake of hooves. Our lantern's little orange flare.

Made a round mask of our each sleep-dazed face,
Bodiless, or else bodies by horses
That whinnied and bit and cannoned the world from its place.

The tall palace was so white, the moon was so round,
Everything else this plunging of horses
To the rim of our eyes that strove for the shapes of the sound.

We crouched at our lantern, our bodies drank the din,
And we longed for a death trampled by such horses
As every grain of the earth had hooves and mane.

We must have fallen like drunkards into a dream
Of listening, lulled by the thunder of the horses.
We awoke stiff; broad day had come.

Out through the gate the unprinted desert stretched
To stone and scorpion; our stable-horses
Lay in their straw, in a hag-sweat, listless and wretched.

Now let us, tied, be quartered by these poor horses,
If but doomsday's flames be great horses,
The forever itself a circling of the hooves of horses.

The poem, by the standard of Hughes's best writing, is not all that good; it is less controlled than Larkin's and has a number of romantic, quasi-medieval trappings which verge on the pretentious. But it is unquestionably *about* something; it is a serious attempt to re-create and so clarify, unfalsified and in the strongest imaginative terms possible, a powerful complex of emotions and sensations. Unlike Larkin's, Hughes's horses have a violent, impending presence. But through the sharp details which bring them so threateningly to life, they reach back, as in a dream, into a nexus of fear and sensation. Their brute world is part physical, part state of mind.

They have, of course, their literary antecedents: the strange, savage horses which terrorize Ursula Brangwen at the end of *The Rainbow*. But this is part of their wider significance. Dr Leavis has come, apparently, to believe that D. H. Lawrence and T. S. Eliot represent the two warring and unreconcilable poles of modern literature. The best contemporary English verse, however, shows that their influences can be creatively reconciled. In the seriousness of what I have called the new depth poetry, the openness to experience, the psychological insight and integrity of D. H. Lawrence would, ideally, combine with the technical skill and formal intelligence of T. S. Eliot. If this were to happen, we would have contemporary work which, like Coleridge's Imagination, would reconcile 'a more than usual state of emotion with more than usual order'.

My own feeling is that a good deal of poetic talent exists in England at the moment. But whether or not it will come to anything largely depends not on the machinations of any literary racket but on the degree to which the poets can remain immune to the disease so often found in English culture: gentility.

A. ALVAREZ

# THE AMERICANS

## JOHN BERRYMAN

### *The Statue*

THE statue, tolerant through years of weather,
Spares the untidy Sunday throng its look,
Spares shopgirls knowledge of the fatal pallor
Under their evening colour,
Spares homosexuals, the crippled, the alone,
Extravagant perception of their failure;
Looks only, cynical, across them all
To the delightful Avenue and its lights.

Where I sit, near the entrance to the Park,
The charming dangerous entrance to their need,
Dozens, a hundred men have lain till morning
And the preservative darkness waning,
Waking to want, to the day before, desire
For the ultimate good, Respect, to hunger waking;
Like the statue ruined but without its eyes;
Turned vaguely out at dawn for a new day.

Fountains I hear behind me on the left,
See green, see natural life springing in May
To spend its summer sheltering our lovers,
Those walks so shortly to be over.
The sound of water cannot startle them
Although their happiness runs out like water,
Of too much sweetness the expected drain.
They trust their Spring; they have not seen the
  statue.

Disfigurement is general. Nevertheless
Winters have not been able to alter its pride,
If that expression is a pride ramaining,
Coriolanus and Rome burning,
An aristocracy that moves no more.
Scholars can stay their pity; from the ceiling
Watch blasted and superb inhabitants,
The sleepless justifying ruined stare.

Since graduating from its years of flesh
The name has faded in the public mind
Or doubled: which is this? the elder? younger?
The statesman or the traveller?
Who first died or who edited his works,
The lonely brother bound to remain longer
By a quarter-century than the first-born
Of that illustrious and lost family?

The lovers pass. Not one of them can know
Or care which Humboldt is immortalized.
If they glance up, they glance in passing,
An idle outcome of that pacing
That never stops, and proves them animal;
These thighs breasts pointed eyes are not their
  choosing,
But blind insignia by which are known
Season, excitement, loosed upon this city.

Turning: the brilliant Avenue, red, green,
The laws of passage; marvellous hotels;
Beyond, the dark apartment where one summer
Night an insignificant dreamer,
Defeated occupant, will close his eyes
Mercifully on the expensive drama
Wherein he wasted so much skill, such faith,
And salvaged less than the intolerable statue.

JOHN BERRYMAN

# *The Moon and the Night and the Men*

ON the night of the Belgian surrender the moon rose
Late, a delayed moon, and a violent moon
For the English or the American beholder;
The French beholder. It was a cold night,
People put on their wraps, the troops were cold
No doubt, despite the calendar, no doubt
Numbers of refugees coughed, and the sight
Or sound of some killed others. A cold night.

On Outer Drive there was an accident:
A stupid well-intentioned man turned sharp
Right and abruptly he became an angel
Fingering an unfamiliar harp,
Or screamed in hell, or was nothing at all.
Do not imagine this is unimportant.
He was a part of the night, part of the land,
Part of the bitter and exhausted ground
Out of which memory grows.

Michael and I
Stared at each other over chess, and spoke
As little as possible, and drank and played.
The chessmen caught in the European eye,
Neither of us I think had a free look
Although the game was fair. The move one made
It was difficult at last to keep one's mind on.
'. . . hurt and unhappy' said the man in London.
We said to each other, The time is coming near
When none shall have books or music, none his dear,
And only a fool will speak aloud his mind.
History is approaching a speechless end,
As Henry Adams said. Adams was right.

All this occurred on the night when Leopold
Fulfilled the treachery four years before

Begun – or was he well-intentioned, more
Roadmaker to hell than king? At any rate,
The moon came up late and the night was cold,
Many men died – although we know the fate
Of none, nor of anyone, and the war
Goes on, and the moon in the breast of man is cold.

## *The Ball Poem*

WHAT is the boy now, who has lost his ball,
What, what is he to do? I saw it go
Merrily bouncing, down the street, and then
Merrily over – there it is in the water!
No use to say 'O there are other balls':
An ultimate shaking grief fixes the boy
As he stands rigid, trembling, staring down
All his young days into the harbour where
His ball went. I would not intrude on him,
A dime, another ball, is worthless. Now
He senses first responsibility
In a world of possessions. People will take balls,
Balls will be lost always, little boy,
And no one buys a ball back. Money is external.
He is learning, well behind his desperate eyes,
The epistemology of loss, how to stand up
Knowing what every man must one day know
And most know many days, how to stand up.
And gradually light returns to the street,
A whistle blows, the ball is out of sight,
Soon part of me will explore the deep and dark
Floor of the harbour . . . I am everywhere,
I suffer and move, my mind and my heart move
With all that move me, under the water
Or whistling, I am not a little boy.

## *The Song of the Tortured Girl*

AFTER a little I could not have told –
But no one asked me this – why I was there.
I asked. The ceiling of that place was high
And there were sudden noises, which I made.
I must have stayed there a long time today:
My cup of soup was gone when they brought me
  back.

Often 'Nothing worse now can come to us'
I thought, the winter the young men stayed away,
My uncle died, and mother cracked her crutch.
And then the strange room where the brightest light
Does not shine on the strange men: shines on me.
I feel them stretch my youth and throw a switch.

Through leafless branches the sweet wind blows
Making a mild sound, softer than a moan;
High in a pass once where we put our tent,
Minutes I lay awake to hear my joy.
– I no longer remember what they want.–
Minutes I lay awake to hear my joy.

## *Whether there is Sorrow in the Demons*

NEAR the top a bad turn some dare. Well,
The horse swerves and screams, his eyes pop,
Feet feel air, the firm winds prop
Jaws wide wider until
Through great teeth rider greets the smiles of Hell.

Thick night, where the host's thews crack like thongs
A welcome, curving abrupt on cheek & neck.
No wings swing over once to check
Lick of their fire's tongues,
Whip & chuckle, hoarse insulting songs.

Powers immortal, fixed, intractable.
Only the lost soul jerks whom they joy hang:
Clap of remorse, and tang and fang
More frightful than the drill
An outsize dentist scatters down a skull;

Nostalgia rips him swinging. Fast in malice
How may his masters mourn, how ever yearn
The frore pride wherein they burn?
God's fire. To what *qui tollis*
Stone-tufted ears prick back towards the bright
  Palace?

Whence Lucifer shone Lucifer's friends hail
The scourge of choice made at the point of light
Destined into eternal night;
Motionless to fulfil
Their least, their envy looks up dense and pale.

. . . Repine blackmarket felons; murderers
Sit still their time, till yellow feet go first,
Dies soon in them, and can die, thirst;
Not lives in these, nor years
On years scar their despair – which yet rehearse . . .

Their belvedere is black. They believe, and quail.
One shudder racks them only, lonely, and
No mirror cracks at their command.
Unsocketed, their will
Grinds on their fate. So was, so shall be still.

## *New Year's Eve*

THE grey girl who had not been singing stopped,
And a brave new no-sound blew through acrid air.
I set my drink down, hard. Somebody slapped

Somebody's second wife somewhere,
Wheeling away to long to be alone.
I see the dragon of years is almost done,
Its claws loosen, its eyes
Crust now with tears & lust and a scale of lies.

A whisky-listless and excessive saint
Was expounding his position, whom I hung
Boy-glad in glowing heaven: he grows faint:
Hearing what song the sirens sung,
Sidelong he web-slid and some rich prose spun.
The tissue golden of the gifts undone
Surpassed the gifts. Miss Weirs
Whispers to me her international fears.

Intelligentsia milling. In a semi-German
(Our loss of Latin fractured how far our fate, –
Disinterested once, linkage once like a sermon)
I struggle to articulate
Why it is our promise breaks in pieces early.
The Muses' visitants come soon, go surly
With liquor & mirrors away
In this land wealthy & casual as a holiday.

Whom the Bitch winks at. Most of us are linsey-
woolsey workmen, grandiose, and slack.
*On m'analyse*, the key to secrets. Kinsey
Shortly will tell us sharply back
Habits we stuttered. How revive to join
(Great evils grieve beneath: eye Caesar's coin)
And lure a while more home
The vivid wanderers, uneasy with our shame?

Priests of the infinite! ah, not for long.
The dove whispers, and diminishes
Up the blue leagues. And no doubt we heard
  wrong –

Wax of our lives collects & dulls; but was
What we heard hurried as we memorized,
Or brightened, or adjusted? Undisguised
We pray our tongues & fingers
Record the strange word that blows suddenly and
  lingers.

Imagine a patience in the works of love
Luck sometimes visits. Ages we have sighed,
And cleave more sternly to a music of
Even this sore word 'genocide'.
Each to his own! Clockless & thankless dream
And labour Makers, being what we seem.
Soon O enough we turn
Our tools in; brownshirt Time chiefly our works
  will burn.

I remember: white fine flour everywhere whirled
Ceaselessly, wheels rolled, a slow thunder boomed,
And there were snowy men in the mill-world
With sparkling eyes, light hair uncombed,
And one of them was humming an old song,
Sack upon sack grew portly, until strong
Arms moved them on, by pairs,
And then the bell clanged and they ran like hares.

Scotch in his oxter, my Retarded One
Blows in before the midnight; freezing slush
Stamps off, off. Worst of years! . . . no matter,
  begone;
Your slash and spells (in the sudden hush)
We see now we had to suffer some day, so
I cross the dragon with a blessing, low,
While the black blood slows. Clock-wise,
We clasp upon the stroke, kissing with happy cries.

## from *Homage to Mistress Bradstreet*

17

THE winters close, Springs open, no child stirs
under my withering heart, O seasoned heart
God grudged his aid.
All things else soil like a shirt.
Simon is much away. My executive stales.
The town came through for the cartway by the
pales,
but my patience is short,
I revolt from, I am like, these savage foresters

18

whose passionless dicker in the shade, whose glance
impassive & scant, belie their murderous cries
when quarry seems to show.
Again I must have been wrong, twice.
Unwell in a new way. Can that begin?
God brandishes. O love, O I love. Kin,
gather. My world is strange
and merciful, ingrown months, blessing a swelling
trance.

19

So squeezed, wince you I scream? I love you & hate
off with you. Ages! *Useless*. Below my waist
he has me in Hell's vice.
Stalling. He let go. Come back: brace
me somewhere. No. No. Yes! everything down
hardens I press with horrible joy down
my back cracks like a wrist
shame I am voiding oh behind it is too late

20

hide me forever I work thrust I must free
now I all muscles & bones concentrate

what is living from dying?
Simon I must leave you so untidy
Monster you are killing me Be sure
I'll have you later Women do endure
I cań *can* no longer
and it passes the wretched trap whelming and I
  am me

21

drencht & powerful, I did it with my body!
One proud tug greens Heaven. Marvellous,
unforbidding Majesty.
Swell, imperious bells. I fly.
Mountainous, woman not breaks and will bend:
sways God nearby: anguish comes to an end.
Blossomed Sarah, and I
blossom. Is that thing alive? I hear a famisht howl.

## ROBERT LOWELL

### *The Quaker Graveyard in Nantucket*

I

A BRACKISH reach of shoal off Madaket –
The sea was still breaking violently and night
Had steamed into our North Atlantic Fleet,
When the drowned sailor clutched the drag-net. Light
Flashed from his matted head and marble feet,
He grappled at the net
With the coiled, hurdling muscles of his thighs:
The corpse was bloodless, a botch of reds and whites,
Its open, staring eyes
Were lustreless dead-lights
Or cabin-windows on a stranded hulk
Heavy with sand. We weight the body, close
Its eyes and heave it seaward whence it came,
Where the heel-headed dogfish barks its nose
On Ahab's void and forehead; and the name
Is blocked in yellow chalk,
Sailors, who pitch this portent at the sea
Where dreadnoughts shall confess
Its hell-bent deity,
When you are powerless
To sand-bag this Atlantic bulwark, faced
By the earth-shaker, green, unwearied, chaste
In his steel scales: ask for no Orphean lute
To pluck life back. The guns of the steeled fleet
Recoil and then repeat
The hoarse salute.

II

Whenever winds are moving and their breath
Heaves at the roped-in bulwarks of this pier,
The terns and sea-gulls tremble at your death

In these home waters. Sailor, can you hear
The Pequod's sea wings, beating landward, fall
Headlong and break on our Atlantic wall
Off 'Sconset, where the yawing S-boats splash
The bellbuoy, with ballooning spinnakers,
As the entangled, screeching mainsheet clears
The blocks: off Madaket, where lubbers lash
The heavy surf and throw their long lead squids
For blue-fish? Sea-gulls blink their heavy lids
Seaward. The winds' wings beat upon the stones,
Cousin, and scream for you and the claws rush
At the sea's throat and wring it in the slush
Of this old Quaker graveyard where the bones
Cry out in the long night for the hurt beast
Bobbing by Ahab's whaleboats in the East.

III

All you recovered from Poseidon died
With you, my cousin, and the harrowed brine
Is fruitless on the blue beard of the god,
Stretching beyond us to the castles in Spain,
Nantucket's westward haven. To Cape Cod
Guns, cradled on the tide,
Blast the eelgrass about a waterclock
Of bilge and backwash, roil the salt and sand
Lashing earth's scaffold, rock
Our warships in the hand
Of the great God, where time's contrition blues
Whatever it was these Quaker sailors lost
In the mad scramble of their lives. They died
When time was open-eyed,
Wooden and childish; only bones abide
There, in the nowhere, where their boats were tossed
Sky-high, where mariners had fabled news
Of IS, the whited monster. What it cost
Them is their secret. In their monster's slick
I see the Quakers drown and hear their cry:

'If God himself had not been on our side,
If God himself had not been on our side,
When the Atlantic rose against us, why,
Then it had swallowed us up quick.'

IV

This is the end of the whaleroad and the whale
Who spewed Nantucket bones on the thrashed swell
And stirred the troubled waters to whirlpools
To send the Pequod packing off to hell:
This is the end of them, three-quarters fools,
Snatching at straws to sail
Seaward and seaward on the turntail whale,
Spouting out blood and water as it rolls,
Sick as a dog to these Atlantic shoals:
*Clamavimus*, O depths. Let the sea-gulls wail

For water, for the deep where the high tide
Mutters to its hurt self, mutters and ebbs.
Waves wallow in their wash, go out and out,
Leave only the death-rattle of the crabs,
The beach increasing, its enormous snout
Sucking the ocean's side.
This is the end of running on the waves;
We are poured out like water. Who will dance
The mast-lashed master of Leviathans
Up from this field of Quakers in their unstoned graves?

V

When the whale's viscera go and the roll
Of its corruption overruns this world
Beyond tree-swept Nantucket and Wood's Hole
And Martha's Vineyard, Sailor, will your sword
Whistle and fall and sink into the fat?
In the great ash-pit of Jehoshaphat

The bones cry for the blood of the white whale,
The fat flukes arch and whack about its ears,
The death-lance churns into the sanctuary, tears
The gun-blue swingle, heaving like a flail,
And hacks the coiling life out: it works and drags
And rips the sperm-whale's midriff into rags,
Gobbets of blubber spill to wind and weather,
Sailor, and gulls go round the stoven timbers
Where the morning stars sing out together
And thunder shakes the white surf and dismembers
The red flag hammered in the mast-head. Hide,
Our steel, Jonas Messias, in Thy side.

VI

## OUR LADY OF WALSINGHAM

There once the penitents took off their shoes
And then walked barefoot the remaining mile;
And the small trees, a stream and hedgerows file
Slowly along the munching English lane,
Like cows to the old shrine, until you lose
Track of your dragging pain.
The stream flows down under the druid tree,
Shiloah's whirlpools gurgle and make glad
The castle of God. Sailor, you were glad
And whistled Sion by that stream. But see:

Our Lady, too small for her canopy,
Sits near the altar. There's no comeliness
At all or charm in that expressionless
Face with its heavy eyelids. As before,
This face, for centuries a memory,
*Non est species, neque decor,*
Expressionless, expresses God: it goes
Past castled Sion. She knows what God knows,
Not Calvary's Cross nor crib at Bethlehem
Now, and the world shall come to Walsingham.

VII

The empty winds are creaking and the oak
Splatters and splatters on the cenotaph,
The boughs are trembling and a gaff
Bobs on the untimely stroke
Of the greased wash exploding on a shoal-bell
In the old mouth of the Atlantic. It's well;
Atlantic, you are fouled with the blue sailors,
Sea-monsters, upward angel, downward fish:
Unmarried and corroding, spare of flesh
Mart once of supercilious, wing'd clippers,
Atlantic, where your ball-trap guts its spoil
You could cut the brackish winds with a knife
Here in Nantucket, and cast up the time
When the Lord God formed man from the sea's slime
And breathed into his face the breath of life,
And blue-lung'd combers lumbered to the kill.
The Lord survives the rainbow of His will.

## *France*

(from *The Gibbet*)

MY human brothers who live after me,
See how I hang. My bones eat through the skin
And flesh they carried here upon the chin
And lipping clutch of their cupidity;
Now here, now there, the starling and the sea
Gull splinter the groined eyeballs of my sin,
Brothers, more beaks of birds than needles in
The fathoms of the Bayeux Tapestry:
'God wills it, wills it, wills it: it is blood.'
My brothers, if I call you brothers, see:
The blood of Abel crying from the dead
Sticks to my blackened skull and eyes. What good
Are *lebensraum* and bread to Abel dead
And rotten on the cross-beams of the tree?

## *Mr Edwards and the Spider*

I SAW the spiders marching through the air,
Swimming from tree to tree that mildewed day
In latter August when the hay
Came creaking to the barn. But where
The wind is westerly,
Where gnarled November makes the spiders fly
Into the apparitions of the sky,
They purpose nothing but their ease and die
Urgently beating east to sunrise and the sea;

What are we in the hands of the great God?
It was in vain you set up thorn and briar
In battle array against the fire
And treason crackling in your blood;
For the wild thorns grow tame
And will do nothing to oppose the flame;
Your lacerations tell the losing game
You play against a sickness past your cure.
How will the hands be strong? How will the heart
endure?

A very little thing, a little worm,
Or hourglass-blazoned spider, it is said,
Can kill a tiger. Will the dead
Hold up his mirror and affirm
To the four winds the smell
And flash of his authority? It's well
If God who holds you to the pit of hell,
Much as one holds a spider, will destroy,
Baffle and dissipate your soul. As a small boy

On Windsor Marsh, I saw the spider die
When thrown into the bowels of fierce fire:
There's no long struggle, no desire
To get up on its feet and fly –

It stretches out its feet
And dies. This is the sinner's last retreat;
Yes, and no strength exerted on the heat
Then sinews the abolished will, when sick
And full of burning, it will whistle on a brick.

But who can plumb the sinking of that soul?
Josiah Hawley, picture yourself cast
Into a brick-kiln where the blast
Fans your quick vitals to a coal –
If measured by a glass,
How long would it seem burning! Let there pass
A minute, ten, ten trillion; but the blaze
Is infinite, eternal: this is death,
To die and know it. This is the Black Widow,
   death.

## *Waking in the Blue*

THE night attendant, a B.U. sophomore,
rouses from the mare's-nest of his drowsy head
propped on *The Meaning of Meaning*
He catwalks down our corridor.
Azure day
makes my agonized blue window bleaker.
Crows maunder on the petrified fairway.
Absence! My heart grows tense
as though a harpoon were sparring for the kill.
(This is the house for the 'mentally ill'.)

What use is my sense of humour?
I grin at 'Stanley', now sunk in his sixties,
once a Harvard all-American fullback,
(if such were possible!)
still hoarding the build of a boy in his twenties,
as he soaks, a ramrod
with the muscle of a seal

in his long tub,
vaguely urinous from the Victorian plumbing.
A kingly granite profile in a crimson golf-cap,
worn all day, all night,
he thinks only of his figure,
of slimming on sherbet and ginger ale –
more cut off from words than a seal.

This is the way day breaks in Bowditch Hall at
McLean's;
the hooded night lights bring out 'Bobbie',
Porcellian '29,
a replica of Louis XVI
without the wig –
redolent and roly-poly as a sperm whale,
as he swashbuckles about in his birthday suit
and horses at chairs.

These victorious figures of bravado ossified young.

In between the limits of day,
hours and hours go by under the crew haircuts
and slightly too little nonsensical bachelor twinkle
of the Roman Catholic attendants.
(There are no Mayflower
screwballs in the Catholic Church.)

After a hearty New England breakfast,
I weigh two hundred pounds
this morning. Cock of the walk,
I strut in my turtle-necked French sailor's jersey
before the metal shaving mirrors,
and see the shaky future grow familiar
in the pinched, indigenous faces
of these thoroughbred mental cases,
twice my age and half my weight.
We are all old-timers,
each of us holds a locked razor.

## *Man and Wife*

TAMED by *Miltown*, we lie on Mother's bed;
the rising sun in war paint dyes us red;
in broad daylight her gilded bed-posts shine,
abandoned, almost Dionysian.
At last the trees are green on Marlborough Street,
blossoms on our magnolia ignite
the morning with their murderous five days' white.
All night I've held your hand,
as if you had
a fourth time faced the kingdom of the mad –
its hackneyed speech, its homicidal eye –
and dragged me home alive . . . Oh my *Petite*,
clearest of all God's creatures, still all air and nerve:
you were in your twenties, and I,
once hand on glass
and heart in mouth,
outdrank the Rahvs in the heat
of Greenwich Village, fainting at your feet –
too boiled and shy
and poker-faced to make a pass,
while the shrill verve
of your invective scorched the traditional South.

Now twelve years later, you turn your back.
Sleepless, you hold
your pillow to your hollows like a child,
your old-fashioned tirade –
loving, rapid, merciless –
breaks like the Atlantic Ocean on my head.

## *'To Speak of the Woe that is in Marriage'*

***'It is the future generation that presses into being by means of these exuberant feelings and supersensible soap bubbles of ours.'***

SCHOPENHAUER

'THE hot night makes us keep our bedroom
windows open.
Our magnolia blossoms. Life begins to happen.
My hopped up husband drops his home disputes,
and hits the streets to cruise for prostitutes,
free-lancing out along the razor's edge.
This screwball might kill his wife, then take the
pledge.
Oh the monotonous meanness of his lust . . .
It's the injustice . . . he is so unjust –
whisky-blind, swaggering home at five.
My only thought is how to keep alive.
What makes him tick? Each night now I tie
ten dollars and his car key to my thigh. . . .
Gored by the climacteric of his want,
he stalls above me like an elephant.'

## *Skunk Hour*

(For Elizabeth Bishop)

NAUTILUS Island's hermit
heiress still lives through winter in her Spartan
cottage;
her sheep still graze above the sea.
Her son's a bishop. Her farmer
is first selectman in our village,
she's in her dotage.

Thirsting for
the hierarchic privacy
of Queen Victoria's century,

she buys up all
the eyesores facing her shore,
and lets them fall.

The season's ill –
we've lost our summer millionaire,
who seemed to leap from an L.L. Bean
catalogue. His nine-knot yawl
was auctioned off to lobstermen.
A red fox stain covers Blue Hill.

And now our fairy
decorator brightens his shop for fall,
his fishnet's filled with orange cork,
orange, his cobbler's bench and awl,
there is no money in his work,
he'd rather marry.

One dark night,
my Tudor Ford climbed the hill's skull,
I watched for love-cars. Lights turned down,
they lay together, hull to hull,
where the graveyard shelves on the town...
My mind's not right.

A car radio bleats,
'Love, O careless Love...' I hear
my ill-spirit sob in each blood cell,
as if my hand were at its throat...
I myself am hell,
nobody's here –

only skunks, that search
in the moonlight for a bite to eat.
They march on their soles up Main Street:
white stripes, moonstruck eyes' red fire
under the chalk-dry and spar spire
of the Trinitarian Church.

I stand on top
of our back steps and breathe the rich air –
a mother skunk with her column of kittens swills
  the garbage pail.
She jabs her wedge-head in a cup
of sour cream, drops her ostrich tail
and will not scare.

## ANNE SEXTON

### *You, Doctor Martin*

YOU, Doctor Martin, walk
from breakfast to madness. Late August,
I speed through the antiseptic tunnel
where the moving dead still talk
of pushing their bones against the thrust
of cure. And I am queen of this summer hotel
or the laughing bee on a stalk

of death. We stand in broken
lines and wait while they unlock
the door and count us at the frozen gates
of dinner. The shibboleth is spoken
and we move to gravy in our smock
of smiles. We chew in rows, our plates
scratch and whine like chalk

in school. There are no knives
for cutting your throat. I make
moccasins all morning. At first my hands
kept empty, unravelled for the lives
they used to work. Now I learn to take
them back, each angry finger that demands
I mend what another will break

tomorrow. Of course, I love you;
you lean above the plastic sky,
god of our block, prince of all the foxes.
The breaking crowns are new
that Jack wore. Your third eye
moves among us and lights the separate boxes
where we sleep or cry.

What large children we are
here. All over I grow most tall
in the best ward. Your business is people,
you call at the madhouse, an oracular
eye in our nest. Out in the hall
the intercom pages you. You twist in the pull
of the foxy children who fall

like floods of life in frost.
And we are magic talking to itself,
noisy and alone. I am queen of all my sins
forgotten. Am I still lost?
Once I was beautiful. Now I am myself,
counting this row and that row of moccasins
waiting on the silent shelf.

## *Elizabeth Gone*

YOU lay in the nest of your real death,
Beyond the print of my nervous fingers
Where they touched your moving head;
Your old skin puckering, your lungs' breath
Grown baby short as you looked up last
At my face swinging over the human bed,
And somewhere you cried, *let me go let me go*.

You lay in the crate of your last death,
But were not you, not finally you.
They have stuffed her cheeks, I said;
This clay hand, this mask of Elizabeth
Are not true. From within the satin
And the suede of this inhuman bed,
Something cried, *let me go let me go*.

II

They gave me your ash and bony shells,
Rattling like gourds in the cardboard urn,
Rattling like stones that their oven had blest.
I waited you in the cathedral of spells
And I waited you in the country of the living
Still with the urn crooned to my breast,
When something cried, *let me go let me go.*

So I threw out your last bony shells
And heard me scream for the look of you,
Your apple face, the simple crèche
Of your arms, the August smells
Of your skin. Then I sorted your clothes
And the loves you had left, Elizabeth,
Elizabeth, until you were gone.

## *Her Kind*

I HAVE gone out, a possessed witch,
haunting the black air, braver at night;
dreaming evil, I have done my hitch
over the plain houses, light by light:
lonely thing, twelve-fingered, out of mind.
A woman like that is not a woman, quite.
I have been her kind.

I have found the warm caves in the woods,
filled them with skillets, carvings, shelves,
closets, silks, innumerable goods;
fixed the suppers for the worms and the elves:
whining, rearranging the disaligned.
A woman like that is misunderstood.
I have been her kind.

I have ridden in your cart, driver,
waved my nude arms at villages going by,

learning the last bright routes, survivor
where your flames still bite my thigh
and my ribs crack where your wheels wind.
A woman like that is not ashamed to die.
I have been her kind.

## *The Abortion*

*Somebody who should have been born*
*is gone.*

JUST as the earth puckered its mouth,
each bud puffing out from its knot,
I changed my shoes, and then drove south.

Up past the Blue Mountains, where
Pennsylvania humps on endlessly,
wearing, like a crayoned cat, its green hair,

its roads sunken in like a grey washboard;
where, in truth, the ground cracks evilly,
a dark socket from which the coal has poured,

*Somebody who should have been born*
*is gone.*

the grass as bristly and stout as chives,
and me wondering when the ground would
  break,
and me wondering how anything fragile
  survives;

up in Pennsylvania, I met a little man,
not Rumpelstiltskin, at all, at all . . .
he took the fullness that love began.

Returning north, even the sky grew thin
like a high window looking nowhere.
The road was as flat as a sheet of tin,

*Somebody who should have been born*
*is gone.*

Yes, woman, such logic will lead
to loss without death. Or say what you meant,
you coward . . . this baby that I bleed.

## *For God While Sleeping*

SLEEPING in fever, I am unfit
to know just who you are:
hung up like a pig on exhibit,
the delicate wrists,
the beard drooling blood and vinegar;
hooked to your own weight,
jolting toward death under your nameplate.

Everyone in this crowd needs a bath.
I am dressed in rags.
The mother wears blue. You grind your teeth
and with each new breath
your jaws gape and your diaper sags.
I am not to blame
for all this. I do not know your name.

Skinny man, you are somebody's fault.
You ride on dark poles –
a wooden bird that a trader built
for some fool who felt
that he could make the flight. Now you roll
in your sleep, seasick
on your own breathing, poor old convict.

## *Old*

I'M afraid of needles,
I'm tired of rubber sheets and tubes.
I'm tired of faces that I don't know
and now I think that death is starting.
Death starts like a dream,
full of objects and my sister's laughter.
We are young and we are walking
and picking wild blueberries
all the way to Damariscotta.
Oh Susan, she cried,
you've stained your new waist.
Sweet taste –
my mouth so full
and the sweet blue running out
all the way to Damariscotta.
What are you doing? Leave me alone!
Can't you see I'm dreaming?
In a dream you are never eighty.

SYLVIA PLATH

## *Lady Lazarus*

I HAVE done it again.
One year in every ten
I manage it –

A sort of walking miracle, my skin
Bright as a Nazi lampshade,
My right foot

A paperweight,
My face a featureless, fine
Jew linen.

Peel off the napkin
O my enemy.
Do I terrify? –

The nose, the eye pits, the full set of
  teeth?
The sour breath
Will vanish in a day.

Soon, soon the flesh
The grave cave ate will be
At home on me

And I a smiling woman.
I am only thirty.
And like the cat I have nine times to die.

This is Number Three.
What a trash
To annihilate each decade.

What a million filaments.
The peanut-crunching crowd
Shoves in to see

Them unwrap me hand and foot –
The big strip tease.
Gentlemen, ladies

These are my hands
My knees.
I may be skin and bone,

Nevertheless, I am the same, identical
  woman.
The first time it happened I was ten.
It was an accident.

The second time I meant
To last it out and not come back at all.
I rocked shut

As a seashell.
They had to call and call
And pick the worms off me like sticky pearls.

Dying
Is an art, like everything else.
I do it exceptionally well.

I do it so it feels like hell.
I do it so it feels real.
I guess you could say I've a call.

It's easy enough to do it in a cell.
It's easy enough to do it and stay put.
It's the theatrical

Comeback in broad day
To the same place, the same face,
 the same brute
Amused shout:

'A miracle!'
That knocks me out.
There is a charge

For the eyeing of my scars, there is a
 charge
For the hearing of my heart –
It really goes.

And there is a charge, a very large charge
For a word or a touch
Or a bit of blood

Or a piece of my hair or my clothes.
So, so, Herr Doktor.
So, Herr Enemy.

I am your opus,
I am your valuable,
The pure gold baby

That melts to a shriek.
I turn and burn.
Do not think I underestimate your
 great concern.

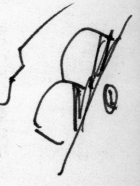

Ash, ash –
You poke and stir.
Flesh, bone, there is nothing there –

A cake of soap,
A wedding ring,
A gold filling.

Herr God, Herr Lucifer
Beware
Beware.

Out of the ash
I rise with my red hair
And I eat men like air.

## *Daddy*

YOU do not do, you do not do
Any more, black shoe
In which I have lived like a foot
For thirty years, poor and white,
Barely daring to breathe or Achoo.

Daddy, I have had to kill you.
You died before I had time –
Marble-heavy, a bag full of God,
Ghastly statue with one grey toe
Big as a Frisco seal

And a head in the freakish Atlantic
Where it pours bean green over blue
In the waters off beautiful Nauset.
I used to pray to recover you.
Ach, du.

In the German tongue, in the Polish town
Scraped flat by the roller
Of wars, wars, wars.
But the name of the town is common.
My Polack friend

Says there are a dozen or two.
So I never could tell where you
Put your foot, your root,

I never could talk to you.
The tongue stuck in my jaw.

It stuck in a barb wire snare.
Ich, ich, ich, ich,
I could hardly speak.
I thought every German was you.
And the language obscene

An engine, an engine
Chuffing me off like a Jew.
A Jew to Dachau, Auschwitz, Belsen.
I began to talk like a Jew.
I think I may well be a Jew.

The snows of the Tyrol, the clear beer of
  Vienna
Are not very pure or true.
With my gypsy ancestress and my weird luck
And my Taroc pack and my Taroc pack
I may be a bit of a Jew.

I have always been scared of *you*,
With your Luftwaffe, your gobbledygoo.
And your neat moustache
And your Aryan eye, bright blue.
Panzer-man, panzer-man, O You –

Not God but a swastika
So black no sky could squeak through.
Every woman adores a Fascist,
The boot in the face, the brute
Brute heart of a brute like you.

You stand at the blackboard, daddy,
In the picture I have of you,
A cleft in your chin instead of your foot
But no less a devil for that, no not
Any less the black man who

Bit my pretty red heart in two.
I was ten when they buried you.
At twenty I tried to die
And get back, back, back to you.
I thought even the bones would do.

But they pulled me out of the sack,
And they stuck me together with glue.
And then I knew what to do.
I made a model of you,
A man in black with a Meinkampf look

And a love of the rack and the screw.
And I said I do, I do.
So daddy, I'm finally through.
The black telephone's off at the root,
The voices just can't worm through.

If I've killed one man, I've killed two –
The vampire who said he was you
And drank my blood for a year,
Seven years, if you want to know.
Daddy, you can lie back now.

There's a stake in your fat black heart
And the villagers never liked you.
They are dancing and stamping on you.
They always *knew* it was you.
Daddy, daddy, you bastard, I'm through.

## *The Moon and the Yew Tree*

THIS is the light of the mind, cold and planetary.
The trees of the mind are black. The light is blue.
The grasses unload their griefs on my feet as if I
  were God,
Prickling my ankles and murmuring of their humility.
Fumey, spiritous mists inhabit this place

Separated from my house by a row of headstones.
I simply cannot see where there is to get to.

The moon is no door. It is a face in its own right,
White as a knuckle and terribly upset.
It drags the sea after it like a dark crime; it is quiet
With the O-gape of complete despair. I live here.
Twice on Sunday, the bells startle the sky –
Eight great tongues affirming the Resurrection.
At the end, they soberly bong out their names.

The yew tree points up. It has a Gothic shape.
The eyes lift after it and find the moon.
The moon is my mother. She is not sweet like Mary.
Her blue garments unloose small bats and owls.
How I would like to believe in tenderness –
The face of the effigy, gentled by candles,
Bending, on me in particular, its mild eyes.

I have fallen a long way. Clouds are flowering
Blue and mystical over the face of the stars.
Inside the church, the saints will be all blue,
Floating on their delicate feet over the cold pews,
Their hands and faces stiff with holiness.
The moon sees nothing of this. She is bald and wild.
And the message of the yew tree is blackness –
  blackness and silence.

## *The Arrival of the Bee Box*

I ORDERED this, this clean wood box
Square as a chair and almost too heavy to lift.
I would say it was the coffin of a midget
Or a square baby
Were there not such a din in it.

The box is locked, it is dangerous.
I have to live with it overnight
And I can't keep away from it.

There are no windows, so I can't see what is in
  there.
There is only a little grid, no exit.

I put my eye to the grid.
It is dark, dark,
With the swarmy feeling of African hands
Minute and shrunk for export,
Black on black, angrily clambering.

How can I let them out?
It is the noise that appals me most of all,
The unintelligible syllables.
It is like a Roman mob,
Small, taken one by one, but my god,
  together!

I lay my ear to furious Latin.
I am not a Caesar.
I have simply ordered a box of maniacs.
They can be sent back.
They can die, I need feed them nothing, I am
  the owner.

I wonder how hungry they are.
I wonder if they would forget me
If I just undid the locks and stood back and
  turned into a tree.
There is the laburnum, its blond colonnades,
And the petticoats of the cherry.

They might ignore me immediately
In my moon suit and funeral veil.
I am no source of honey
So why should they turn on me?
Tomorrow I will be sweet God, I will set them
  free.

The box is only temporary.

## *The Swarm*

SOMEBODY is shooting at something in our
town –
A dull pom, pom in the Sunday street.
Jealousy can open the blood,
It can make black roses.
Who are they shooting at?

It is you the knives are out for
At Waterloo, Waterloo, Napoleon,
The hump of Elba on your short back,
And the snow, marshalling its brilliant
cutlery
Mass after mass, saying Shh!

Shh! These are chess people you play with,
Still figures of ivory.
The mud squirms with throats,
Stepping stones for French bootsoles.
The gilt and pink domes of Russia melt
and float off

In the furnace of greed. Clouds, clouds.
So the swarm balls and deserts
Seventy feet up, in a black pine tree.
It must be shot down. Pom! Pom!
So dumb it thinks bullets are thunder.

It thinks they are the voice of God
Condoning the beak, the claw, the grin of
the dog
Yellow-haunched, a pack dog,
Grinning over its bone of ivory
Like the pack, the pack, like everybody.

The bees have got so far. Seventy feet high!
Russia, Poland and Germany!
The mild hills, the same old magenta
Fields shrunk to a penny
Spun into a river, the river crossed.

The bees argue, in their black ball,
A flying hedgehog, all prickles.
The man with grey hands stands under
  the honeycomb
Of their dream, the hived station
Where trains, faithful to their steel arcs,

Leave and arrive, and there is no end to the
  country.
Pom, pom! They fall
Dismembered, to a tod of ivy.
So much for the chariots, the outriders,
  the Grand Army!
A red tatter, Napoleon!

The last badge of victory.
The swarm is knocked into a cocked straw
  hat.
Elba, Elba, bleb on the sea!
The white busts of marshals, admirals,
  generals
Worming themselves into niches.

How instructive this is!
The dumb, banded bodies
Walking the plank draped with Mother
  France's upholstery
Into a new mausoleum,
An ivory palace, a crotch pine.

The man with grey hands smiles –
The smile of a man of business, intensely
  practical.

They are not hands at all
But asbestos receptacles.
Pom, pom! 'They would have killed *me.*'

Stings big as drawing pins!
It seems bees have a notion of honour,
A black, intractable mind.
Napoleon is pleased, he is pleased with
  everything.
O Europe! O ton of honey!

## *Childless Woman*

The womb
Rattles its pod, the moon
Discharges itself from the tree with
  nowhere to go.

My landscape is a hand with no lines,
The roads bunched to a knot,
The knot myself,

Myself the rose you achieve –
This body,
This ivory

Ungodly as a child's shriek.
Spiderlike, I spin mirrors,
Loyal to my image,

Uttering nothing but blood –
Taste it, dark red!
And my forest

My funeral,
And this hill and this
Gleaming with the mouths of corpses.

## *Mary's Song*

THE Sunday lamb cracks in its fat.
The fat
Sacrifices its opacity . . .

A window, holy gold.
The fire makes it precious,
The same fire

Melting the tallow heretics,
Ousting the Jews.
Their thick palls float

Over the cicatrix of Poland, burnt-out
Germany.
They do not die.

Grey birds obsess my heart,
Mouth-ash, ash of eye.
They settle. On the high

Precipice
That emptied one man into space
The ovens glowed like heavens,
incandescent.

It is a heart,
This holocaust I walk in,
O golden child the world will kill
and eat.

# THE BRITISH

## NORMAN MacCAIG

### *Particular You*

  WHAT question will unmask
The hooded rose-tree, upright in its shadow?
Or show the steadiness that makes the stone steady?
  Or, knowing it, who would dare to ask
And change the pretty phenomena into one
Horde of disclosures blackening the sun?

  Reveal to me no more
Than what I know of you – your bright disguises.
The lie your body is only discloses
  The language of a rose-tree or
A stone; and universals gather where
Your hands lie still or light falls on your hair.

  But you are more and less
Than universals. I'd tremble to discover
That special, stubborn thing, that must forever
  Lie hooded between no and yes,
An affirmation which must always be
Incomprehensible and separate from me.

  I study to be wise.
Lift up the lesson of your hand. Then, gazing,
I lose the loss of what I must be losing
  And find the language of disguise
Says all I want and bear to know, that we
And all the world are three, but one in three.

## *Gifts*

YOU read the old Irish poet and complain
I do not offer you impossible things –
Gloves of bee's fur, cap of the wren's wings,
Goblets so clear light falls on them like a stain,
I make you the harder offer of all I can,
The good and ill that make of me this man.

I need no fancy to mark you as beautiful,
If you are beautiful. All I know is what
Darkens and brightens the sad waste of my thought
Is what makes me your wild, truth-telling fool
Who will not spoil your power by adding one
Vainglorious image to all we've said and done.

Flowers need no fantasy, stones need no dream:
And you are flower and stone. And I compel
Myself to be no more than possible,
Offering nothing that might one day seem
A measure of your failure to be true
To the greedy vanity that disfigures you.

A cloak of the finest silk in Scotland – what
Has that to do with troubled nights and days
Of sorry happiness? I had no praise
Even of your kindness, that was not bought
At such a price this bankrupt self is all
I have to give. And is that possible?

## *Feeding Ducks*

ONE duck stood on my toes.
The others made watery rushes after bread
Thrown by my momentary hand; instead
She stood duck-still and got far more than those.

An invisible drone boomed by
With a beetle in it; the neighbour's yearning bull
Bugled across five fields. And an evening full
Of other evenings quietly began to die.

And my everlasting hand
Dropped on my hypocrite duck her grace of bread.
And I thought, 'The first to be fattened, the first
to be dead',
Till my gestures enlarged, wide over the
darkening land.

## *Spate in Winter Midnight*

THE streams fall down and through the darkness bear
Such wild and shaking hair,
Such looks beyond a cool surmise,
Such lamentable uproar from night skies
As turn the owl from honey of blood and make
Great stags stand still to hear the darkness shake.

Through Troys of bracken and Babel towers of rocks
Shrinks now the looting fox,
Fearful to touch the thudding ground
And flattened to it by the mastering sound.
And roebuck stilt and leap sideways; their skin
Twitches like water on the fear within.

Black hills are slashed white with this falling grace.
Whose violence buckles space
To a sheet-iron thunder. This
Is noise made universe, whose still centre is
Where the cold adder sleeps in his small bed.
Curled neatly round his neat and evil head.

## *Mutual Life*

A WILDCAT, fur-fire in a bracken bush,
Twitches his club-tail, rounds his amber eyes
At rockabye rabbits humped on the world. The air
Crackles about him. His world is a rabbit's size.

And in milky pearls, in a liquefaction of green,
One of ten thousand, spattering squabs of light,
A mackerel shuttles the hanging waterwebs,
Muscling through tons, slipping them left and right.

What do you know, mind, of that speck in air,
The high, insanitary raven that pecks his claws
A thousand feet up and volplanes on his back
And greets his ancient sweetheart with coarse caws?

You tell a hand to rise and you think it yours.
It makes a shape (you have none) in a space
It gives perspective to. You sink in it
And disappear there, foundered without trace.

And dreadful alienations bring you down
Into a proper loneliness. You cry
For limits that make a wildcat possible
And laws that tumble ravens in the sky.

Till clenched hand opens, drowning into you,
Where mackerel, wildcat, raven never fall
Out of their proper spaces; and you are
Perpetual resurrection of them all.

## *A Peasant*

IAGO PRYTHERCH his name, though, be it allowed,
Just an ordinary man of the bald Welsh hills,
Who pens a few sheep in a gap of cloud.
Docking mangels, chipping the green skin
From the yellow bones with a half-witted grin
Of satisfaction, or churning the crude earth
To a stiff sea of clods that glint in the wind –
So are his days spent, his spittled mirth
Rarer than the sun that cracks the cheeks
Of the gaunt sky perhaps once in a week.
And then at night see him fixed in his chair
Motionless, except when he leans to gob in the fire.
There is something frightening in the vacancy of his
mind.
His clothes, sour with years of sweat
And animal contact, shock the refined,
But affected, sense with their stark naturalness.
Yet this is your prototype, who, season by season
Against siege of rain and the wind's attrition,
Preserves his stock, an impregnable fortress
Not to be stormed even in death's confusion.
Remember him then, for he, too, is a winner of wars,
Enduring like a tree under the curious stars.

## *The Welsh Hill Country*

TOO far for you to see
The fluke and the foot-rot and the fat maggot
Gnawing the skin from the small bones,
The sheep are grazing at Bwlch-y-Fedwen,
Arranged romantically in the usual manner
On a bleak background of bald stone.

Too far for you to see
The moss and the mould on the cold chimneys,
The nettles growing through the cracked doors,
The houses stand empty at Nant-yr-Eira,
There are holes in the roofs that are thatched with
    sunlight,
And the fields are reverting to the bare moor.

Too far, too far to see
The set of his eyes and the slow phthisis
Wasting his frame under the ripped coat,
There's a man still farming at Ty'n-y-Fawnog,
Contributing grimly to the accepted pattern,
The embryo music dead in his throat.

## *Welsh Landscape*

To live in Wales is to be conscious
At dusk of the spilled blood
That went to the making of the wild sky,
Dyeing the immaculate rivers
In all their courses.
It is to be aware,
Above the noisy tractor
And hum of the machine
Of strife in the strung woods,
Vibrant with sped arrows,
You cannot live in the present,
At least not in Wales.
There is the language for instance,
The soft consonants
Strange to the ear.
There are cries in the dark at night
As owls answer the moon,
And thick ambush of shadows,

Hushed at the fields' corners
There is no present in Wales,
And no future;
There is only the past,
Brittle with relics,
Wind-bitten towers and castles
With sham ghosts;
Mouldering quarries and mines;
And an impotent people,
Sick with inbreeding,
Worrying the carcase of an old song.

## *Song at the Year's Turning*

SHELLEY dreamed it. Now the dream decays.
The props crumble. The familiar ways
Are stale with tears trodden underfoot.
The heart's flower withers at the root.
Bury it, then, in history's sterile dust.
The slow years shall tame your tawny lust.

Love deceived him; what is there to say
The mind brought you by a better way
To this despair? Lost in the world's wood
You cannot stanch the bright menstrual blood.
The earth sickens; under naked boughs
The frost comes to barb your broken vows.

Is there blessing? Light's peculiar grace
In cold splendour robes this tortured place
For strange marriage. Voices in the wind
Weave a garland where a mortal sinned.
Winter rots you; who is there to blame?
The new grass shall purge you in its flame.

## *January*

THE fox drags its wounded belly
Over the snow, the crimson seeds
Of blood burst with a mild explosion,
Soft as excrement, bold as roses.

Over the snow that feels no pity,
Whose white hands can give no healing,
The fox drags its wounded belly.

## *Evans*

EVANS? Yes, many a time
I came down his bare flight
Of stairs into the gaunt kitchen
With its wood fire, where crickets sang
Accompaniment to the black kettle's
Whine, and so into the cold
Dark to smother in the thick tide
Of night that drifted about the walls
Of his stark farm on the hill ridge.

It was not the dark filling my eyes
And mouth appalled me; not even the drip
Of rain like blood from the one tree
Weather-tortured. It was the dark
Silting the veins of that sick man
I left stranded upon the vast
And lonely shore of his bleak bed.

## *A Blackbird Singing*

IT seems wrong that out of this bird,
Black, bold, a suggestion of dark

Places about it, there yet should come
Such rich music, as though the notes'
Ore were changed to a rare metal
At one touch of that bright bill.

You have heard it often, alone at your desk
In a green April, your mind drawn
Away from its work by sweet disturbance
Of the mild evening outside your room.

A slow singer, but loading each phrase
With history's overtones, love, joy
And grief learned by his dark tribe
In other orchards and passed on
Instinctively as they are now,
But fresh always with new tears.

## *On a Line in Sandburg*

'Where did the blood come from?
Before I bit, before I sucked
The red meat, the blood was there
Nourishing sweetly the roots of hair.'

'The blood came from your mother
By way of the long gut-cord;
You were the pain in her side;
You were born on a blood-dark tide.'

'My mother also was young
Once, but her cheeks were red
Even then. From its hidden source
The hot blood ran on its old course.

Where did the blood come from?'

## *Here*

I AM a man now.
Pass your hand over my brow:
You can feel the place where the brains grow.

I am like a tree:
From my top boughs I can see
The footprints that led up to me.

There is blood in my veins
That has run clear of the stain
Contracted in so many loins.

Why, then, are my hands red
With the blood of so many dead?
Is this where I was misled?

Why are my hands this way
That they will not do as I say?
Does no God hear when I pray?

I have nowhere to go.
The swift satellites show
The clock of my whole being is slow.

It is too late to start
For destinations not of the heart.
I must stay here with my hurt.

## *Walter Llywarch*

I AM, as you know, Walter Llywarch,
Born in Wales of approved parents,
Well goitred, round in the bum;
Sure prey of the slow virus
Bred in quarries of grey rain.

Born in autumn at the right time
For hearing stories from the cracked lips
Of old folk dreaming of summer,
I piled them on to the bare hearth
Of my own fancy to make a blaze
To warm myself, but achieved only
The smoke's acid that brings the smart
Of false tears into the eyes.

Months of fog, months of drizzle:
Thought wrapped in the grey cocoon
Of race, of place, awaiting the sun's
Coming; but when the sun came,
Striking the hills with a hot hand,
Wings were spread only to fly
Round and round in a cramped cage,
Or beat in vain at the sky's window.

School in the week; on Sunday chapel:
Tales of a land fairer than this
Were not so tall, for others had proved it
Without the grave's passport; they sent
Its fruit home for ourselves to taste. . . .

Walter Llywarch! The words were the name
On a lost letter that never came
For one who waited in the long queue
Of life that wound through a Welsh valley.
I took instead, as others had done
Before, a wife from the back pew
In chapel, rather to share the rain
Of winter evenings than to intrude
On her pale body. And yet we lay
For warmth together and laughed to hear
Each new child's cry of despair.

## D. J. ENRIGHT

### *Sightseeing*

ALONG the long wide temple wall
Extends a large and detailed painting.

A demon's head, its mouth square open,
Inside the mouth a room of people squatting.

Its fangs the polished pillars of the room,
The crimson carpet of the floor its tongue.

Inside this room a painting on the wall,
A demon's head, its mouth square open.

Inside the mouth a room of people squatting,
Their faces blank, the artist did not care.

Inside that room a painting on the wall,
A demon's head, its mouth square open.

Somewhere you are squatting, somewhere there.
Imagination, like the eyes that strain

Against the wall, is happily too weak
To number all the jaws there are to slip.

### *A Polished Performance*

CITIZENS of the polished capital
  Sigh for the towns up country,
And their innocent simplicity.

People in the towns up country
  Applaud the unpolished innocence
Of the distant villages.

Dwellers in the distant villages
  Speak of a simple unspoilt girl,
Living alone, deep in the bush.

Deep in the bush we found her,
  Large and innocent of eye,
Among gentle gibbons and mountain ferns.

Perfect for the part, perfect,
  Except for the dropsy
Which comes from polished rice.

In the capital our film is much admired,
  Its gentle gibbons and mountain ferns,
Unspoilt, unpolished, large and innocent of eye.

## *The Poor Wake Up Quickly*

SURPRISED at night,
The trishaw driver
Slithers from the carriage,
Hurls himself upon the saddle.

With what violence he peddles
Slapbang into the swarming night,
Neon skidding off his cheekbones!
Madly he makes away
In the wrong direction.
I tap his shoulder nervously.
Madly he turns about
Between the taxis and the trams,
Makes away electric-eyed
In another wrong direction.

How do I star in that opium dream?
A hulking red-faced ruffian
Who beats him on his bony back,
Cursing in the tongue of demons.

But when we're there
He grumbles mildly over his wage,
Like a sober man,
A man who has had no recent visions.
The poor wake up quickly.

## *The Noodle-Vendor's Flute*

In a real city, from a real house,
At midnight by the ticking clocks,
In winter by the crackling roads:
Hearing the noodle-vendor's flute,
Two single fragile falling notes . . .
But what can this small sing-song say,
Under the noise of war?
The flute itself a counterfeit
(Siberian wind can freeze the lips),
Merely a rubber bulb and metal horn
(Hard to ride a cycle, watch for manholes
And late drunks, and play a flute together).
Just squeeze between gloved fingers,
And the note of mild hope sounds:
Release, the indrawn sigh of mild despair . . .
A poignant signal, like the cooee
Of some diffident soul locked out,
Less than appropriate to cooling macaroni.
Two wooden boxes slung across the wheel,
A rider in his middle age, trundling
This gross contraption on a dismal road,
Red eyes and nose and breathless rubber horn.
Yet still the pathos of that double tune
Defies its provenance, and can warm
The bitter night.
Sleepless, we turn and sleep.
Or sickness dwindles to some local limb.

Bought love for one long moment gives itself.
Or there a witch assures a frightened child
She bears no personal grudge.
And I, like other listeners,
See my stupid sadness as a common thing.
And being common,
Therefore something rare indeed.
The puffing vendor, surer than a trumpet,
Tells us we are not alone.
Each night that same frail midnight tune
Squeezed from a bogus flute,
Under the noise of war, after war's noise,
It mourns the fallen, every night,
It celebrates survival –
In real cities, real houses, real time.

### *The Proper Due*

A THIN willow hovers here:
Lovely – lovely in spite of
The thick drain oozing near
Between sick banks, a vein of evil.

Lovely because of . . .
For acres of willows look like nothing.
Beauty defines itself against the dirt,
That telling reflection –
Like health against a hurt –
Deep in the dark infection.

Hell is easy to foretell –
Mud without the willow,
Shallow silence with not a single bell,
Still shadow of exhausted monologue.

Hard to envisage Heaven –
Acres of willows, haloes in eternal floodlights,
Ten thousand harps that keep in time?

Our best imagination: sights,
  Free and frequent, of the distant slime.

  So one returns to earth, to see again
The willow, and to pay the filth its proper due.
  That in the end – the very end – one vision
Grows from two.

## *Saying No*

AFTER so many (in so many places) words,
It came to this one, No.
Epochs of parakeets, of peacocks, of paradisiac birds –
Then one bald owl croaked, No.

And now (in this one place, one time) to celebrate,
One sound will serve.
After the love-laced talk of art, philosophy and fate –
Just, No.

Some virtue here, in this speech-stupefied inane,
To keep it short.
However, cumbrous, puffed and stretched the pain –
To say no more than, No.

Virtue (or only decency) it would have been,
But – no.
I dress that death's head, all too plain, too clean,
With lots of pretty lengths of saying,

No.

## *The Quagga*

BY mid-century there were two quaggas left,
And one of the two was male.
The cares of office weighed heavily on him.

When you are the only male of a species,
It is not easy to lead a normal sort of life.

The goats nibbled and belched in casual content;
They charged and skidded up and down their concrete
mountain.
One might cut his throat on broken glass,
Another stray too near the tigers.
But they were zealous husbands; and the enclosure was
always full,
Its rank air throbbing with ingenuous voices.

The quagga, however, was a man of destiny.
His wife, whom he had met rather late in her life,
Preferred to sleep, or complain of the food and the
weather.
For their little garden was less than paradisiac,
With its artificial sun that either scorched or left you cold,
And savants with cameras eternally hanging around,
To perpetuate the only male quagga in the world.

Perhaps that was why he failed to do it himself.
It is all very well for goats and monkeys –
But the last male of a species is subject to peculiar
pressures.
If ancient Satan had come slithering in, perhaps . . .
But instead the savants, with cameras and notebooks,
Writing sad stories of the decadence of quaggas.

And then one sultry afternoon he started raising Cain.
This angry young quagga kicked the bars and broke a
camera;
He even tried to bite his astonished keeper.
He protested loud and clear against this and that,
Till the other animals became quite embarrassed
For he seemed to be calling them names.

Then he noticed his wife, awake with the noise,
And a curious feeling quivered round his belly.

He was Adam: there was Eve.
Galloping over to her, his head flung back,
He stumbled, and broke a leg, and had to be shot.

## *The Laughing Hyena, by Hokusai*

For him, it seems, everything was molten. Court ladies
flow in gentle streams,
Or, gathering lotus, strain sideways from their curving
boat,
A donkey prances, or a kite dances in the sky, or soars like
sacrificial smoke.
All is flux: waters fall and leap, and bridges leap and fall.
Even his Tortoise undulates, and his Spring Hat is lively as
a pool of fish.
All he ever saw was sea: a sea of marble splinters –
Long bright fingers claw across his pages, fjords and
islands and shattered trees –

And the Laughing Hyena, cavalier of evil, as volcanic as
the rest:
Elegant in a flowered gown, a face like a bomb-burst,
Featured with fangs and built about a rigid laugh,
Ever moving, like a pond's surface where a corpse has
sunk.
Between the raised talons of the right hand rests an
object –
At rest, like a pale island in a savage sea – a child's head,
Immobile, authentic, torn and bloody –
The point of repose in the picture, the point of movement
in us.

Terrible enough, this demon. Yet it is present and perfect,
Firm as its horns, curling among its thick and handsome
hair.

I find it an honest visitant, even consoling, after all
Those sententious phantoms, choked with rage and
uncertainty,
Who grimace from contemporary pages. It, at least,
Knows exactly why it laughs.

## *On the Death of a Child*

THE greatest griefs shall find themselves inside the
smallest cage.
It's only then that we can hope to tame their rage,

The monsters we must live with. For it will not do
To hiss humanity because one human threw
Us out of heart and home. Or part

At odds with life because one baby failed to live.
Indeed, as little as its subject, is the wreath we give –

The big words fail to fit. Like giant boxes
Round small bodies. Taking up improper room,
Where so much withering is, and so much bloom.

## *Apocalypse*

'After the New Apocalypse, very few members were still in possession of their instruments. Hardly a musician could call a decent suit his own. Yet, by the early summer of 1945, strains of sweet music floated on the air again. While the town still reeked of smoke, charred buildings and the stench of corpses, the Philharmonic Orchestra bestowed the everlasting and imperishable joy which music never fails to give.'

*(From 'The Muses on the Banks of the Spree',*
*a German tourist brochure)*

IT soothes the savage doubts.
One Bach outweighs ten Belsens. If 200,000 people

Were remaindered at Hiroshima, the sales of So-and-So's
New novel reached a higher figure in as short a time.
So, imperishable paintings reappeared;
Texts were reprinted;
Public buildings reconstructed;
Human beings reproduced.

After the Newer Apocalypse, very few members
Were still in possession of their instruments
(Very few were still in possession of their members),
And their suits were chiefly indecent.
Yet, while the town still reeked of smoke etc.,
The Philharmonic Trio bestowed etc.

A civilization vindicated,
A race with three legs still to stand on!
True, the violin was later silenced by leukaemia,
And the pianoforte crumbled softly into dust.
But the flute was left. And one is enough.
All, in a sense, goes on. All is in order.

And the ten-tongued mammoth larks,
The forty-foot crickets and the elephantine frogs
Decided that the little chap was harmless,
At least he made no noise, on the banks of whatever river
  it used to be.

One day, a reed-warbler stepped on him by accident.
However, all, in a sense, goes on. Still the everlasting and
  imperishable joy
Which music never fails to give is being given.

## DONALD DAVIE

### *Time Passing, Beloved*

TIME passing, and the memories of love
Coming back to me, carissima, no more mockingly
Than ever before; time passing, unslackening,
Unhastening, steadily; and no more
Bitterly, beloved, the memories of love
Coming into the shore.

How will it end? Time passing, and our passages of
love
As ever, beloved, blind
As ever before; time binding, unbinding
About us; and yet to remember
Never less chastening, nor the flame of love
Less like an ember.

What will become of us? Time
Passing, beloved, and we in a sealed
Assurance unassailed
By memory. How can it end,
This siege of a shore that no misgivings have steeled,
No doubts defend?

### *Dream Forest*

THESE have I set up,
Types of ideal virtue,
To be authenticated
By no one's Life and Times,
But by a sculptor's logic

Of whom I have commanded,
To dignify my groves,

Busts in the antique manner,
Each in the space mown down
Under its own sway:

First, or to break the circle,
Brutus, imperious, curbed
Not much by the general will,
But by a will to be curbed,
A preference for limits;

Pushkin next, protean
Who recognized no checks
Yet brooked them all – a mind
Molten and thereby fluent,
Unforced, easily strict;

The next, less fortunate,
Went honourably mad,
The angry annalist
Of hearth and marriage bed,
Strindberg – a staring head.

Classic, romantic, realist,
These have I set up.
These have I set, and a few trees.
When will a grove grow over
This mile upon mile of moor?

## *The Mushroom Gatherers*

(after Mickiewicz)

STRANGE walkers! See their processional
Perambulations under low boughs,
The birches white, and the green turf under.
These should be ghosts by moonlight wandering.

Their attitudes strange: the human tree
Slowly revolves on its bole. All around
Downcast looks; and the direct dreamer
Treads out in trance his lane, unwavering.

Strange decorum: so prodigal of bows,
Yet lost in thought and self-absorbed, they meet
Impassively, without acknowledgement.
A courteous nation, but unsociable.

Field full of folk, in their immunity
From human ills, crestfallen and serene.
Who would have thought these shades our lively
    friends?
Surely these acres are Elysian Fields.

## *Under St Paul's*

WREN and Barry, Rennie and Mylne and Dance
Under the flags, the men who stood for stone
Lie in the stone. Carillons, pigeons once
Sluiced Ludgate's issues daily, and the dome
Of stone-revetted crystal swung and hung
Its wealth of waters. Wren had plugged it home
With a crypt at the nerve of London. Now the gull
Circles the dry stone nozzles of the belfries,
Each graceful City hydrant of the full
Eagerly brimming measure of agreement,
Still to be tapped by any well-disposed
Conversible man, still underneath the pavement
Purling and running, affable and in earnest,
The conduit, Candour. Fattily urbane
Under the great drum, pigeons foul their nest.

The whiter wing, Anger, and the gull's
Shearwater raucous over hunting hulls

Seek London's river. Rivers underground,
Under the crypt, return the sound
Of footfalls in the evening city. Out of wells,
Churchyards sunk behind Fleet Street, trickle smells
Of water where a calm conviction spoke
Now dank and standing. Leaves and our debris choke
The bell-note Candour that the paviour heard
Fluting and swelling like a crop-filled bird.

Suppose those tides, from under a masonry shelf
With great white blind fish, float into sunlight
From a dark behind Candour, darkness of love itself;
Conviction's claim still holds us, to deny
Nothing that's undeniable. Light airs
Are bent to the birds that couple as they fly
And slide and soar, yet answer to the flow
Of this broad water under. There we ride
Lent to the current, and convictions grow
In those they are meant for. As Conviction's face
Is darker than the speculative air,
So and no darker is the place
For Candour and Love. What fowl lives underwater,
Breeds in that dark? And hadn't a contriver
Of alphabets, Cadmus, the gull for daughter?

Across the dark face of the waters
Flies the white bird. And the waters
Mount, mount, or should mount; we grow surer
Of what we know, if no surer
Of what we think. For on ageing
Labouring now and subsiding and nerveless wing
The gull sips the body of water, and the air
Packed at that level can hold up a minster in air.
Across the dark face of the water
Flies the white bird until nothing is left but the water.

## DONALD DAVIE

### *Epilogue*

(after Mickiewicz)

HOW many memories, what long sorrow
There where a man shall cleave to his master
As here no wife cleaves to her man;
There where a man grieves for loss of his weapons
Longer than here for who sired him;
And his tears fall more sincerely and faster
There for a hound than this people's for heroes.

My friends of those days made my speech come
    easy,
Each good for some singable idiom. Spring
Brought in the fable cranes of the wild island flying
Over the spellbound castle and the spellbound
Boy lamenting, who was loosed
By each pitying bird as it flew, one feather:
He flew out on those wings to his own people.

## PHILIP LARKIN

### *Wedding Wind*

The wind blew all my wedding-day,
And my wedding-night was the night of the high
  wind;
And a stable door was banging, again and again,
That he must go and shut it, leaving me
Stupid in candlelight, hearing rain,
Seeing my face in the twisted candlestick,
Yet seeing nothing. When he came back
He said the horses were restless, and I was sad
That any man or beast that night should lack
The happiness I had.

            Now in the day
All's ravelled under the sun by the wind's blowing.
He has gone to look at the floods, and I
Carry a chipped pail to the chicken-run,
Set it down, and stare. All is the wind
Hunting through clouds and forests, thrashing
My apron and the hanging cloths on the line.
Can it be borne, this bodying-forth by wind
Of joy my actions turn on, like a thread
Carrying beads? Shall I be let to sleep
Now this perpetual morning shares my bed?
Can even death dry up
These new delighted lakes, conclude
Our kneeling as cattle by all-generous waters?

PHILIP LARKIN

## *Poetry of Departures*

SOMETIMES you hear, fifth-hand,
As epitaph:
*He chucked up everything*
*And just cleared off,*
And always the voice will sound
Certain you approve
This audacious, purifying,
Elemental move.

And they are right, I think.
We all hate home
And having to be there:
I detest my room,
Its specially-chosen junk,
The good books, the good bed,
And my life, in perfect order:
So to hear it said

*He walked out on the whole crowd*
Leaves me flushed and stirred,
Like *Then she undid her dress*
Or *take that you bastard*;
Surely I can, if he did?
And that helps me stay
Sober and industrious.
But I'd go today,

Yes, swagger the nut-strewn roads,
Crouch in the fo'c'sle
Stubbly with goodness, if
It weren't so artificial,
Such a deliberate step backwards
To create an object:
Books; china; a life
Reprehensibly perfect.

It's idiomatic familiarity of tone is in many ways typical of recent British poetry.



more use & acceptance of colloquialism, even slang.

## *Toads*

Why should I let the toad *work*
  Squat on my life?
Can't I use my wit as a pitchfork
  And drive the brute off?

Six days of the week it soils
  With its sickening poison –
Just for paying a few bills!
  That's out of proportion.

Escape from banality.

Lots of folk live on their wits:
  Lecturers, lispers,
Losels, loblolly-men, louts –
  They don't end as paupers;

Lots of folk live up lanes
  With fires in a bucket,
Eat windfalls and tinned sardines –
  They seem to like it.

Their nippers have got bare feet,
  Their unspeakable wives
Are skinny as whippets – and yet
  No one actually *starves*.

Ah, were I courageous enough
  To shout *Stuff your pension*!
But I know, all too well, that's the stuff
  That dreams are made on:

For something sufficiently toad-like
  Squats in me, too;
Its hunkers are heavy as hard luck,
  And cold as snow,

And will never allow me to blarney
  My way to getting
The fame and the girl and the money
  All at one sitting.

I don't say, one bodies the other
One's spiritual truth;
But I do say it's hard to lose either,
When you have both.

## *If, My Darling*

If my darling were once to decide
Not to stop at my eyes,
But to jump, like Alice, with floating skirt into my head,

She would find no tables and chairs,
No mahogany claw-footed sideboards,
No undisturbed embers;

The tantalus would not be filled, nor the fender-seat cosy,
Nor the shelves stuffed with small-printed books for the Sabbath,
Nor the butler bibulous, the housemaids lazy:

She would find herself looped with the creep of varying light,
Monkey-brown, fish-grey, a string of infected circles
Loitering like bullies, about to coagulate;

Delusions that shrink to the size of a woman's glove,
Then sicken inclusively outwards. She would also remark
The unwholesome floor, as it might be the skin of a grave,

From which ascends an adhesive sense of betrayal,
A Grecian statue kicked in the privates, money,
A swill-tub of finer feelings. But most of all

She'd be stopping her ears against the incessant recital
Intoned by reality, larded with technical terms,
Each one double-yolked with meaning and meaning's rebuttal:

For the skirl of that bulletin unpicks the world like a knot,
And to hear how the past is past and the future neuter
Might knock my darling off her unpriceable pivot.

## *Going*

THERE is an evening coming in
Across the fields, one never seen before,
That lights no lamps.

Silken it seems at a distance, yet
When it is drawn up over the knees and breast
It brings no comfort.

Where has the tree gone, that locked
Earth to the sky? What is under my hands,
That I cannot feel?

What loads my hands down?

## *Wants*

BEYOND all this, the wish to be alone:
However the sky grows dark with invitation-card
However we follow the printed directions of sex
However the family is photographed under the
flagstaff –
Beyond all this, the wish to be alone.

Beneath it all, desire of oblivion runs:
Despite the artful tensions of the calendar,
The life insurance, the tabled fertility rites,
The costly aversion of the eyes from death –
Beneath it all, desire of oblivion runs.

# *The Whitsun Weddings*

THAT Whitsun, I was late getting away:
    Not till about
One-twenty on the sunlit Saturday
Did my three-quarters-empty train pull out,
All windows down, all cushions hot, all sense
Of being in a hurry gone. We ran
Behind the backs of houses, crossed a street
Of blinding windscreens, smelt the fish-dock; thence
The river's level drifting breadth began,
Where sky and Lincolnshire and water meet.

All afternoon, through the tall heat that slept
    For miles inland,
A slow and stopping curve southwards we kept.
Wide farms went by, short-shadowed cattle, and
Canals with floatings of industrial froth;
A hothouse flashed, uniquely; hedges dipped
And rose; and now and then a smell of grass
Displaced the reek of buttoned carriage-cloth
Until the next town, new and nondescript,
Approached with acres of dismantled cars.

At first, I didn't notice what a noise
    The weddings made
Each station that we stopped at: sun destroys
The interest of what's happening in the shade,
And down the long cool platforms whoops and skirls
I took for porters larking with the mails
And went on reading. Once we started, though,
We passed them, grinning and pomaded, girls
In parodies of fashion, heels and veils,
All posed irresolutely, watching us go,

As if out on the end of an event
        Waving good-bye
To something that survived it. Struck, I leant
More promptly out next time, more curiously,
And saw it all again in different terms:
The fathers with broad belts under their suits
And seamy foreheads: mothers loud and fat;
An uncle shouting smut; and then the perms,
The nylon gloves and jewellery-substitutes,
The lemons, mauves, and olive-ochres that

Marked off the girls unreally from the rest.
        Yes, from cafés
And banquet-halls up yards, and bunting-dressed
Coach-party annexes, the wedding-days
Were coming to an end. All down the line
Fresh couples climbed aboard; the rest stood round;
The last confetti and advice were thrown,
And, as we moved, each face seemed to define
Just what it saw departing: children frowned
At something dull; fathers had never known

Success so huge and wholly farcical;
        The women shared
The secret like a happy funeral;
While girls, gripping their handbags tighter, stared
At a religious wounding. Free at last,
And loaded with the sum of all they saw,
We hurried towards London, shuffling gouts of steam.
Now fields were building-plots, and poplars cast
Long shadows over major roads, and for
Some fifty minutes, that in time would seem

Just long enough to settle hats and say
        *I nearly died*
A dozen marriages got under way.
They watched the landscape, sitting side by side
– An Odeon went past, a cooling tower,

And someone running up to bowl – and none
Thought of the others they would never meet
Or how their lives would all contain this hour.
I thought of London spread out in the sun,
Its postal districts packed like squares of wheat:

There we were aimed. And as we raced across
    Bright knots of rail
Past standing Pullmans, walls of blackened moss
Came close, and it was nearly done, this frail
Travelling coincidence; and what it held
Stood ready to be loosed with all the power
That being changed can give. We slowed again,
And as the tightened brakes took hold, there swelled
A sense of falling, like an arrow-shower
Sent out of sight, somewhere becoming rain.

## *Mr Bleaney*

'THIS was Mr Bleaney's room. He stayed
The whole time he was at the Bodies, till
They moved him.' Flowered curtains, thin and
    frayed,
Fall to within five inches of the sill,

Whose window shows a strip of building land,
Tussocky, littered. 'Mr Bleaney took
My bit of garden properly in hand.'
Bed, upright chair, sixty-watt bulb, no hook

Behind the door, no room for books or bags –
'I'll take it.' So it happens that I lie
Where Mr Bleaney lay, and stub my fags
On the same saucer-souvenir, and try

Stuffing my ears with cotton-wool, to drown
The jabbering set he egged her on to buy.
I know his habits – what time he came down,
His preference for sauce to gravy, why

He kept on plugging at the four aways –
Likewise their yearly frame: the Frinton folk
Who put him up for summer holidays,
And Christmas at his sister's house in Stoke.

But if he stood and watched the frigid wind
Tousling the clouds, lay on the fusty bed
Telling himself that this was home, and grinned,
And shivered, without shaking off the dread

That how we live measures our own nature,
And at his age having no more to show
Than one hired box should make him pretty sure
He warranted no better, I don't know.

## KINGSLEY AMIS

### *Beowulf*

So, bored with dragons, he lay down to sleep,
Locking for good his massive hoard of words
(Discuss and illustrate), forgetting now
The hope of heathens, muddled thoughts on fate.

Councils would have to get along without him:
The peerless prince had taken his last bribe
(*Lif is læne*) useless now the byrnie
Hard and hand-locked, fit for a baseball catcher.

Only with Grendel was he man-to-man;
Grendel's dam was his only sort of woman
(Weak conjugation). After they were gone
How could he stand the bench-din, the yelp-word?

Someone has told us this man was a hero.
Must we then reproduce his paradigms,
Trace out his rambling regress to his forbears
(An instance of Old English harking-back)?

### *Dirty Story*

TWICE daily, at noon and dusk, if we are lucky,
We hear fresh news of you, an oral cutting
From your unlimited biography.

Today a butcher, you cuckolded the grocer,
Fouling his sugar, in thirty seconds only,
All the while tickling a pretty customer;

Yesterday you posed as a winking parson
Or a gull from the north, cloaking your belly-
laughter
With a false voice that mourned for what you'd
done;

Tomorrow, in what shrines gaily excreting,
Will you, our champion even if defeated,
Bring down a solemn edifice with one swing?

Hero of single action, epic expert,
Beggar prince and bandit chief of the sexy,
Spry Juan, lifter of the lifted skirt,

What is the secret of your howling successes –
Your tongue never tardy with the punch sentence,
Your you-know-what in fabulous readiness?

Is it no more than the researcher's patience
To ransack life's laboratory, and labour
Ten years distilling salts to be used once;

To nose out the precisely suitable landscape,
The curiously jealous, the uniquely randy,
Then blow them all up in a retort or rape?

If so, your exploits should be read in silence,
Words bred of such travail move none to smiling,
But all to an uneasy reverence:

Reverence at such will to live in stories;
Uneasy, because we see behind your glories
Our own nasty defeats, nastier victories.

## *A Dream of Fair Women*

THE door still swinging to, and girls revive,
Aeronauts in the utmost altitudes
Of boredom fainting, dive

Into the bright oxygen of my nod;
Angels as well, a squadron of draped nudes,
  They roar towards their god.

Militant all, they fight to take my hat,
No more as yet; the other men retire
  Insulted, gestured at;
Each girl presses on me her share of what
Makes up the barn-door target of desire:
  And I am a crack shot.

Speech fails them, amorous, but each one's look,
Endorsed in other ways, begs me to sign
  Her body's autograph-book;
'Me first, Kingsley; I'm cleverest' each declares,
But no gourmet races downstairs to dine,
  Nor will I race upstairs.

Feigning aplomb, perhaps for half an hour,
I hover, and am shown by each princess
  The entrance to her tower;
Open, in that its tenant throws the key
At once to anyone, but not unless
  The anyone is me.

Now from the corridor their fathers cheer,
Their brothers, their young men; the cheers increase
  As soon as I appear;
From each I win a handshake and sincere
Congratulations; from the chief of police
  A nod, a wink, a leer.

This over, all delay is over too;
The first eight girls (the roster now agreed)
  Leap on me, and undo . . .
But honesty impels me to confess
That this is 'all a dream', which was, indeed,
  Not difficult to guess.

But wait; not 'just a dream', because, though good
And beautiful, it is also true, and hence
  Is rarely understood;
Who would choose any feasible ideal
In here and now's giant circumference,
  If that small room were real?

Only the best; the others find, have found
Love's ordinary distances too great,
  And, eager, stand their ground;
Map-drunk explorers, dry-land sailors, they
See no arrival that can compensate
  For boredom on the way;

And, seeming doctrinaire, but really weak,
Limelighted dolls guttering in their brain,
  They come with me, to seek
The halls of theoretical delight,
The women of that ever-fresh terrain,
  The night after tonight.

## *Something Nasty in the Bookshop*

BETWEEN the GARDENING and the COOKERY
  Comes the brief POETRY shelf;
By the Nonesuch Donne, a thin anthology
  Offers itself.

Critical, and with nothing else to do,
  I scan the Contents page,
Relieved to find the names are mostly new;
  No one my age.

Like all strangers, they divide by sex:
  *Landscape near Parma*
Interests a man, so does *The Double Vortex*,
  So does *Rilke and Buddha*.

'I travel, you see', 'I think' and 'I can read'
  These titles seem to say;
But *I Remember You, Love is my Creed,*
  *Poem for J.,*

The ladies' choice, discountenance my patter
  For several seconds;
From somewhere in this (as in any) matter
  A moral beckons.

Should poets bicycle-pump the human heart
  Or squash it flat?
Man's love is of man's life a thing apart;
  Girls aren't like that.

We men have got love well weighed up; our stuff
  Can get by without it.
Women don't seem to think that's good enough;
  They write about it,

And the awful way their poems lay them open
  Just doesn't strike them.
Women are really much nicer than men:
  No wonder we like them.

Deciding this, we can forget those times
  We sat up half the night
Chockfull of love, crammed with bright thoughts,
    names, rhymes,
  And couldn't write.

## *The Voice of Authority: A Language Game*

Do this. Don't move. O'Grady says do this,
You get a move on, see, do what I say.
Look lively when I say O'Grady says.

Say this. Shut up. O'Grady says say this,
You talk fast without thinking what to say.
What goes is what I say O'Grady says.

Or rather let me put the point like this:
O'Grady says what goes is what I say
O'Grady says; that's what O'Grady says.

By substituting you can shorten this,
Since any god you like will do to say
The things you like, that's what O'Grady says.

The harm lies not in that, but in that this
Progression's first and last terms are I say
O'Grady says, not just O'Grady says.

Yet it's O'Grady must be out of this
Before what we say goes, not what we say
O'Grady says. Or so O'Grady says.

## DAVID HOLBROOK

### *Poor Old Horse*

A CHILD skipping jump on the quay at the Mill,
With parted legs jump, soft-footed in April,
And the lovers on the bridge, sweet soft women's mouths
Pressing jowls of men, in jeans or loose trousers, youths
Packed in punts. And the masons on the bridge
Pause as they lift white stone to dress the face of the ridge
Of the balustrade, to imagine an actorish man
(Uxorious to a self-possessed blonde) as well as they can,
Back in the hotel room, making love; they laugh,
Turn back to the mortar. Ducks rise over trees, the chaff
Of mixed men and women floats over. A boy with a shiny
  red face
Attentively wipes some beer from his sweetheart's sleeve.
  The place
I remember assignments of old at, by moon and water,
The same acts of living, the same weir-splashed happiness
  after.
But today I sit here alone – with my daughter rather,
Who critically watches the child skipping jump on the
  waterfall quay,
And we after go back to the car. I am dumb, and silent
  she.
I see the spring love on the bridge for her: for me decay,
Or at most the wry pretension, 'Well, we have had our
  day!'
I do not want to have had my day: I do not accept my
  jade,
Any more than the grey old horse we meet in the street,
His shaggy stiff dragged aside for a smart sports blade
And his smart sports car: yet that's no doubt my fate
As the water flows by here each year, April to April,
With a soft-footed child skipping jump on the quay at the
  Mill.

## *Fingers in the Door*

CARELESS for an instant I closed my child's fingers in the
jamb. She
Held her breath, contorted the whole of her being,
foetus-wise, against the
Burning fact of the pain. And for a moment
I wished myself dispersed in a hundred thousand pieces
Among the dead bright stars. The child's cry broke,
She clung to me, and it crowded in to me how she and I
were
Light-years from any mutual help or comfort. For her I
cast seed
Into her mother's womb; cells grew and launched itself as
a being:
Nothing restores her to my being, or ours, even to the
mother who within her
Carried and quickened, bore, and sobbed at her separation,
despite all my envy,
Nothing can restore. She, I, mother, sister, dwell dispersed
among dead bright stars:
We are there in our hundred thousand pieces!

## *Living? Our Supervisors Will Do That For Us!*

DANKWERTS, scholarship boy from the slums,
One of many, studied three years for the Tripos,
Honours, English; grew a beard, imitated the gesture
And the insistent deliberate (but not dogmatic)
'There!' of his supervisor. For a time
The mimesis was startling. Dankwerts knew
Uncannily what was good, what bad.
Life and earning a living, extra muros, for a time
afterwards,

Left him hard up: people in their ambiguity
Nuisances. A bracing need for self-justification
(And spot cash) drove some of the nonsense out of him:
He found a foothold in films, the evening papers,
With his photograph, up to the ears in steaks, or ivy,
In 'art' magazines. Passing over the metropolis
He ejaculates like a satellite, evaporates, and falls,
Albeit on to a fat bank balance of amoral earnings.

Whereas his supervisor can be seen any Friday
Walking up Trumpington Street with an odd movement
of the feet,
Still looking like an old corm, lissom, and knowing
Uncannily what's good, what's bad,
And probably rather hard up out of the bargain.

## *Unholy Marriage*

POLICE ARE SEEKING TO IDENTIFY THE PILLION RIDER WHO WAS ALSO KILLED

HER mother bore her, father cared
And clothed her body, young and neat.
The careful virgin had not shared
Cool soft anointment of her breast
Or any other sweet,
But kept herself for best.

How sweet she would have been in bed,
Her bridegroom sighing in her hair,
His tenderness heaped on her head,
Receiving benediction from her breast
With every other fair
She kept for him, the best.

Who she is now they do not know
Assembling her body on a sheet.

This foolish virgin shared a blow
That drove her almost through a stranger's breast
And all her sweet
Mingles with his in dust.

Unwilling marriage, her blood runs with one
Who bought for a few pounds and pence
A steel machine able to 'do a ton',
Not knowing at a ton a straw will pierce a breast:
No wheel has built-in sense,
Not yet the shiniest and best.

And so, 'doing a ton', in fog and night
Before he could think, Christ! or she could moan
There came a heavy tail without a light
And many tons compressed each back to breast
And blood and brain and bone
Mixed, lay undressed.

Anointed only by the punctured oil
Poured like unleashed wind or fire from bag
Sold by some damned magician out to spoil
The life that girded in this young girl's breast
Now never to unfurl her flag
And march love's happy quest.

Her mother hears the clock; her father sighs,
Takes off his boots: she's late tonight.
I hope she's a careful virgin: men have eyes
For cherished daughters growing in the breast.
Some news? They hear the gate
A man comes: not the best.

## *Reflections on a Book of Reproductions*

HOURS are a small thing, the interior
(Woman at tub, lamps, Vermeer's whore,
Onions or spinets) insignificant

At the time, in Time. But magnificent
The art's consideration of the body,
Nymph bathing; model, now long decayed,
Become Christ off the cross; the maid
Spurning the lover's flowers; old man
Blowing his smoke rings. And if I can
I would lay out the patterns of mine
Into something more than these nine
Hours since I woke this morning, one
For lifting a tree-stump, one to run
A Ford van round the shops for meat,
For onions, for fruit, and the rest we ate;
Another for a child's rest; another
For the two little girls to go to shop with their mother.

Then we all gather round for the tea,
All laying claim to her, or informing me,
Under the candles, about how they bought
A pair of shoes, and how the bus they caught
Struck the branches of trees, and what
The old man in the seat behind
Said to his wife, while they sneezed and grinned.
Yet this is the family food of the aspiration
To celebrate order: Bach's elation
Was nourished on soup and hearth,
And worked among insolent men; the bath
That bathed the Badende Nymphe was crock;
Snyders' lobsters were stolen by cats; the clock
Muttered rustily in their rooms; their studio fires
Went out; cursed their wives, imperfectly fed their
desires;
And the artist would swear at his daughters who sit so
prim
In the Kaiser-Friedrich-Museum, for ever looking at him
With tender and timorous eyes beneath simple crowns of
Flowers:
A Dutch interior is but as clean and simple as ours.

So we are not demeaned by simplicity, or banality,
By our cars, electric kettles, or lamps; the finality
Of our death, even, in the mass-produced chest:
Burial may ennoble us, that we watch our best
From time to time put in the ground. From such roots
We may draw from the soaring elms, the yellow
Pillars of poplar, as each great red ball sinks below
Our pathetic horizon, some share of the significance
The great painters saw, between the small hours and the
natural world's magnificence.

## *Me and the Animals*

I SHARE my kneebones with the gnat,
My joints with ferrets, eyes with rat
Or blind bat, blinking owl, the goat
His golden cloven orb. I mate like a stoat,
Or like the heavy whale, that moves a sea
To make a mother's gross fecundity.

I share lung's action with the snake;
The fish is cold, but vertebrate like me; my steak
Is muscle from a butcher's arm, a butcher's heart
Is some sheep's breast that throbbed; I start
At noise with ears which in a dog
Can hear what I cannot; in water I'm a frog.

I differ most in lacking their content
To be, no more. They're at mercy of the scent,
Of hot, cold, summer, winter, hunger, anger,
Or ritual establishing the herd, smelling out the
stranger:
I walk upright, alone, ungoverned, free:
Yet their occasional lust, fear, unease, walk with me
Always. All ways.

## MICHAEL HAMBURGER

### *Instead of a Journey*

TURN like a top; spin on your dusty axis
Till the bright metal shines again, your head
Hums and the earth accelerates,
Dizzy you drop
Into this easy chair you drowse in daily.
Sit there and watch the walls assume their meaning,
The Chinese plate assert its blue design,
The room renew itself as you grow still.
Then, after your flight and fall, walk to the garden
Or at the open window taste return:
Weather and season, clouds at your vision's rim,
Love's whims, love's habitation, and the heart
By one slow wheel worn down, whetted to gladness.

### *Bird Watcher*

CHALLENGED, he'd say it was a mode of knowing –
As boys in railway stations neutralize a passion
By gathering ciphers: number, date and place –
Yet keeps no record of his rare encounters,
Darkly aware that like his opposite
Who no less deep in woods, as far out on the moors
Makes do with food or trophies, hunts for easy favours,
He trysts defeat by what he cannot know.

'Goldfinch' he says, and means a chirping flutter
From stalk to stalk in early autumn meadows,
Or 'oystercatcher', meaning a high, thin cry
More ghost than bodied voice, articulation
Of the last rock's complaint against the sea.

And wooing with his mind the winter fieldfares
Has made a snare of his binoculars,
For lime and cage and gun has longed in secret,
To kill that he may count, ravish despair
And eat the tongue that will not speak to him,
Though to the wind it speaks, evasive as the wind.

He grows no lighter, they no heavier
As to his mode of loving he returns,
Fixed in the discipline of adoration;
Will keep no pigeons, nor be satisfied
With metropolitan starlings garbling their parodies.

The boy's cold bride will yield, too soon and utterly,
Never these engines fuelled with warm blood,
Graced with peculiar folly that will far outfly him
Till in one communal emptiness they meet.

## *In a Convex Mirror*

A STATELY room – chaise-longue and easy chairs,
Old jugs on carved commodes, a clavichord,
Three landscapes, minor eighteenth century
Against the pale grey walls; and all in half-light,
The street being narrow, the houses opposite tall,
Each with a room like this – a waiting-room.

Sunk in a chair, quite still, a waiting man
Who stares into a classic composition
Heavily framed above the mantelpiece.
A streak of grey, myself in miniature
Against pale pink upholstery, exhales
Invisible smoke; and slowly moves one hand,
Ten minutes only here, half lost already,
Half vanquished by the furniture, half absorbed,
But for the ticking of a clock would yield
All his defences, call the blur delusion.

But 'trumpery' now I mutter, jump up to break it,
Stretch legs not frozen yet, jerk my glazed eyes
Out of this glazed anachronism's eye,
And hear my name called; going, look once more:

A classic composition; nothing stirs.
One little streak of grey that matched the walls
Removed, but in that half-light far too faint
To leave a gap, and soon to be replaced.

## *A Child Accepts*

'LATER,' his mother said; and still those little hands
Clawed air to clutch the object of their need,
Abandoned as birds to winds or fishes to tide,
Pure time that is timeless, time untenanted.

'Later,' she said; and the word was cold with death,
Opposing space to his time, intersecting his will.
He summoned the cry of a wounded animal,
Mindless Adam whose world lies crushed by the Fall,

But suddenly mended his face and far from tears
Grew radiant, relaxed, letting his hands drop down.
'Later,' he sang, and was human, fallen again,
Received into mind, his dubious, his true demesne.

'Later,' he played with the word, and later will envy
The freedom of birds and fishes for ever lost,
When, migrant in mind whom wind and water resist,
Here he must winter in body, bound to the coast;

Or, not all his 'laters' past, perhaps he'll know
That the last releases: reversed, his needs will throng
Homewards to nest in his head and breed among
Those hidden rocks that wrecked him into song.

## *Spring Song in Winter*

Too long, too long
I gathered icicles in spring
To thread them for a melting song;
And in midsummer saw the foliage fall,
Too foolish then to sing
How leaf and petal cling
Though wind would bear them to the root of all.

Now winter's come, and winter proves me wrong:
Dark in my garden the dead,
Great naked briars, have spread,
So vastly multiplied
They almost hide
The single shrub to share whose blossoming
Blood on cold thorns my fingers shed.

## JOHN WAIN

### *The Bad Thing*

Sometimes just being alone seems the bad thing.
Solitude can swell until it blocks the sun.
It hurts so much, even fear, even worrying
Over past and future, get stifled. It has won,
You think; this is the bad thing, it is here.
Then sense comes; you go to sleep, or have
Some food, write a letter or work, get something
 clear.
Solitude shrinks; you are not all its slave.

Then you think: the bad thing inhabits yourself.
Just being alone is nothing; not pain, not balm.
Escape, into poem, into pub, wanting a friend
Is not avoiding the bad thing. The high shelf
Where you stacked the bad thing, hoping for calm,
Broke. It rolled down. It follows you to the end.

### *Poem*

HIPPOLYTUS: Do you see my plight, Queen, stricken as I am?
ARTEMIS: I see. But my eyes are not permitted to shed tears.
EURIPIDES, *Hippolytus*, 1395–6

Like a deaf man meshed in his endless silence
the earth goes swishing through the heaven's wideness.

Doubtless some god with benign inquiring brow
could lean over and let his brown eye so true

play over its whirling scabby hide with a look of searching
till suddenly, with eye and bland forefinger converging

he points to a specially found spot. *Here, this moment*
he might say, *I detect it; this is the locus of torment.*

*This spot is the saddest on earth's entire crust.*
A quaint fancy? Such gods can scarcely exist?

Still, the fact outlives the metaphor it breeds;
whether or not the god exists, the scored earth bleeds.

There must be a point where pain takes its worst hold.
One spot, somewhere, holds the worst grief in the world.

Who would venture a guess as to where this grief lies
    cupped?
Ah, from minute to minute it could never be mapped.

For trouble flies between molecules like a dream.
It flowers from the snapped edge of bones like sour flame.

Who knows what child lies in a night like a mine-shaft
unblinking, his world like a fallen apple mashed and cleft?

Or what failed saint plummets into his private chasm
having bartered all Heaven for one stifling orgasm?

Or perhaps it is even an animal who suffers worst,
gentle furry bundle or two-headed obscene pest.

But where pain's purest drop burns deep no one could say,
unless it were this god with benign brown eye.

Some would curse this god for doing nothing to help.
But he has knowledge like cold water on his scalp.

To perceive that spirit of suffering in its raging purity
is to a god the burden of his divinity.

O then, if he exists, have pity on this god.
He is clamped to that wounded crust with its slime of
    blood.

He has no ignorance to hold him separate.
Everything is known to a god. The gods are desperate.

JOHN WAIN

## *The New Sun*

THE new sun rises in the year's elevation,
over the low roofs' perspective.

It reveals the roughness of winter skin
and the dinginess of winter clothes.

It draws, with a hard forefinger,
a line under the old ways.

*Finis*! the old ways have become obsolete,
the old skin, the old clothes.

This same sun, like a severe comet,
rises over old disappointments.

But how to accept it? is the problem.
How to bear the pain of renewal?

It makes us cry out in agony,
this peeling away of old sorrows.

When the sun foretells the death of an old sorrow,
the heart prophetically feels itself an orphan;

a little snivelling orphan, and the sun
its hard-hearted parish officer.

Dear gods, help us to bear the new sun!
Let our firm hearts pray to be orphaned!

## *Poem Without a Main Verb*

WATCHING oneself
being clever, being clever:
keeping the keen equipoise between *always* and *never;*

delicately divining
(the gambler's sick art)
which of the strands must hold, and which may part;

playing off, playing off
with pointless cunning
the risk of remaining against the risk of running;

balancing balancing
(alert and knowing)
the carelessly hidden with the carefully left showing;

endlessly, endlessly
finely elaborating
the filigree threads in the web and bars in the grating:

at last minutely
and thoroughly lost
in the delta where profit fans into cost;

with superb navigation
afloat on that darkening, deepening sea,
helplessly, helplessly.

JOHN WAIN

## *Au Jardin des Plantes*

THE gorilla lay on his back,
One hand cupped under his head,
Like a man.

Like a labouring man tired with work,
A strong man with his strength burnt away
In the toil of earning a living.

Only of course he was not tired out with work,
Merely with boredom; his terrible strength
All burnt away by prodigal idleness.

A thousand days, and then a thousand days,
Idleness licked away his beautiful strength,
He having no need to earn a living.

It was all laid on, free of charge.
We maintained him, not for doing anything,
But for being what he was.

And so that Sunday morning he lay on his back,
Like a man, like a worn-out man,
One hand cupped under his terrible hard head.

Like a man, like a man,
One of those we maintain, not for doing anything,
But for being what they are.

A thousand days, and then a thousand days,
With everything laid on, free of charge,
They cup their heads in prodigal idleness.

## ARTHUR BOYARS

### *Lovers in a Park*

THE claw protective flung
About her shoulders' haven,
Decrees nor you nor I shall touch
His starveling heaven;

Her stars low sockets hold,
Thin lips her hollow,
Pale tongue through banks of teeth winds where
His love must follow.

Compulsion rears no voice;
In this safe posture
She and her jig-saw man make one,
No green imposture;

Love's animals, though light
Against their barest tender
Mouths shows indifferent flint set to
Indifferent tinder.

And yet no haloes of
Good-byes are spread like dawn
Above her known metropolis,
No moon falls down –

Their paper fingers scorch
Then crinkle, it is still
The same excuse of fire which tempts
Ashes to steal

Their winking heat again:
This is his own version
Of how his others love; a mouse
She smiles, and proves herself his vision.

## ARTHUR BOYARS

### *Horses*

HORSES! Where are these now?
Such sturdy reliables
In a world of the mother,
Here I searched high and low

To find how the prospect could
Turn from so great to so small,
I from a pebble to mountain –
Too soon the flesh faded to wood.

Horses! Where are these now?
Wooden and weak for a brain
Moving heads fixed on pedestals
Carved from dead bough.

How, loving the carved head,
I soon found more life in his
Wooden square-jumping
Than in my giant's cry from the shed;

Prospect lowered, I grew from the earth,
Entered the dark gallery
On tall legs, felt around,
Waited for life and birth.

Face to the glass on the green
Fake of imagined seas,
I watched those wooden manes move
But no legs were seen.

Hoofs and pedestals lost,
What sped their gentility,
Cleaving the dark weed
As their currents crossed?

Only our leap into their
Green day and their wish for our eyes,
Not yet dulled, to trace their descent
From Kings that rode the full air.

## *Initial*

(For Eugenio Montale)

'And so Beatrice became an obsession with Dante'
*New Interpretation*

PASSING out of a great city
A flower in confusion,
I, the speaker, and you, the listener;
You, who would never listen except through words,
Learning with your clay implement,
Moving to change even in daylight,
And I, holding neither the middle way
Of this direction nor any part
Valid for measurement, will lead
Dead Virgil through my private world.

Finding that the wood has not altered,
The Leopard, the Lion
They remain constant, and through them is forward,
And they as unshaken as stone beasts
On the walls, laughing at enemies;
Mating with their bodies after death,
Fruit of a human craftsman;
But He knowing the Hound
From outside, and he with me
Walking equal, the Knowledge and Discord.

How he would come retrieving
Hostages from night,
The way still periculous, overstarred
By new refinements of space: buildings
Settle their grand lumber near incurious skies,
Night blows setting the card
Face downwards, the hand of daylight
Gropes for rescuing fingers,
Finds none, and relapsing slides
Beneath view by its ultimate candle.

The river an eye of bad mirrors
Drawing her face,
A distributed mask on their breaking;
And she, not so much present
As remembered where there is separation
Of whole things: a moment of incaution
And the face gives its relic,
Waits fòr surprise at the move
Waits for its equal, knows none.
Eyes above it. Knowledge and Discord.

I will watch here for the movement,
Not as the ghost
Appears once under lamplight, seen clearly
And then dissolves, a pattern of houses
His backcloth, dwarfed by comparison
Of wires in a no-man's-land: web
On the word as a face stranded
Between spidered branches,
Framed weakly – extending
Without edge. The focus is altered.

Now the somewhere is plain, the rhymes
Run to refuse,
In spite coherence is lost, the names
Of anonymous trees which make this now
Are recalled, the word goes to barter:
Bodies and wheat are ploughed up, the Willow
Remains asserting its sadness;
The last husk of the pearl droops
To dust, her body before me
Emerges a spire to the sun.

This place, this time: all other
Exhausted through love.
Quicksands graze at your harbours,
Shaft at the breakers, tidal, temporary
Report you, too tall for their depth;

On this inner day of the year, fall
Of the meteor cargoed with red veins
Flows branches between, overcoming
Heat, slows the pulse, the Pole-
Star held as a shield.

This time, and the manic dance
Starting differently,
New rhythm of feet, it is You,
New wings to the eye, cone to the heart,
Precipice of lips to the next spending,
And then again. It is not the lights
Of a city, one by one weakening
The roots of feet growing dark, these threads
Cannot bear them: outwards the sand
Wrinkles in the same folds,
And yet differently.

Matching the foot to the furrow,
Unvenomed in Eden,
The short measure divides, music flattens,
A moment, the Queen flashes to cardboard, situations
Flung our wild, paper-decks for a generation.
Silver the serpent uncoils from his tree, silver
Bad mirrors look back; the Lion laying proud paw
On their surface uncovers a head,
It was that dancer they told of,
Water the last valley.

Dead by his own rib. Beatrice
Is Eve with a human
Example: for short pleasure, long displeasure;
It was that dancer, Fantastick, tripping lightly,
Missing the shore he stumbled to deep stones,
Joined with the beast, unexpected
Mingling; bellowed from the maze
To the rampart: 'Is there no sound
Thing that I may devour?' But He with me
Treading equal. Knowledge and Discord.

## *Final Day*

A DOZEN years of days and nights these loved,
Days they were separate, and most nights alone,
Only the evenings made their common home
Where intimacy grew, but this was gloved;
Mouth touching mouth in kiss,
Loins touching loins, but doomed to miss.

They ate the ordinary food, and none complained,
But spoke extraordinary words whose meanings raced
Beyond the langague which had not encased
Such thoughts till then. Words die, but these remained;
Instead of children, better,
Grew up, and were not flesh to fetter.

Only in loneliness; for when food was short
Their private language would unlearn its grace,
And world rushed in with stricken daily face
And made her mouth each pious mundane thought
Which all their life had banished
To beyond, where such thoughts vanished.

Not vanished quite, the ordinary never;
Like fire in flint, its being lay concealed
Till friction for its flame to be revealed,
And famine was the end of this endeavour.
Famine and drought on two mouths lay,
Which, rubbing, set alight their final day.

## *Florence: Garibaldi Day 1949*

NO streets what they say.
No lovers
In the Via dell'Amorino,
No beauties
In the Via delle Belle Donne.

Only
The lovely women
Silent on their shelves,
Flowers before them
Fixed by the lovers of Saints.

And no plenty –
The hands
Stretched out for farthings,
The boys
With imprisoned birds,
While the amorous
Touch
Through blind chinks.

The bridge:
And the jewels
A deception.
Still
Hands grasping
Till the fingers
Reach to the clouds
And pull down
Nightfall.

Death of a day,
The river fades
And the last bird
Moved homeward
In his hungry cage;
This
Fifth of June;

No flag
Concerned with these.

No days
As they call them.

## CHRISTOPHER MIDDLETON

### *At Porthcothan*

A SPECK of dark at low tide on the tideline,
It could not be identified as any known thing
Until, as one approached, a neck was clear
(And it is agreed that logs, or cans, are neckless),
And then a body, over which the neck stood
Curved like a question mark, emerged
As oval, and the whole shape was crouching
Helpless in a small pool the sea had left.

The oval body, with green sheen as of pollen
Shading off into the black plumage, and the neck
Surmounted by the tiny wide-eyed head,
Were not without beauty. The head was moving,
So like a cobra it seemed rash to offer
An introductory finger to the long hooked bill
That stabbed at air. Danger had so
Sharpened what intelligence the bird possessed,
It seemed to pierce the mind of the observer.
In fact we were afraid, yes afraid of each other.

Finally though I picked it up and took it
To a quiet side-bay where dogs were rarer.
Here the shag sat, happy in the sun,
Perched on a slab of rock where a pool was
In which I caught five fish for it
With a pocketknife, a handkerchief
And a plunging forefinger. But at six o'clock
It left the rock and waddled off seaward.

Though breakers came in high and curling
It straddled them, bouncing, buoyant,
Borne along the sealine sideways, with head up,

Slithering across the bay's whole width, and then
Drifted ashore again, to scuttle flapping
With webbed feet flat like a Saturday banker's
To shelter on a level rock. Here it studied,
With the air of one of whom something is expected,
The turbulent Atlantic slowly rising.
What could I do but leave it meditating?

Early next morning on the bay's north side
I found it cuddled under the cliff; the tide
Was low again. What hungry darkness
Had driven so the dark young shag to shelter?
It did not resist when I picked it up.
Something had squeezed the cobra out of it.

I took it to a cave where the sun shone in,
Then caught two fish. It opened one green eye,
And then another. But though I cut
The fish into portions, presenting these
To the bill's hooked tip, it only shook its head.
Noon came. The shag slept in the cave. At two
I hurried back. The shag was stone dead,
With its fine glossy head laid back a little
Over the left shoulder, and a few flies
Were pestering its throat and the fish scraps
Now unlikely to get eaten.

Ten minutes perhaps
I sat there, then carried it up the cliff path
And across the headland to a neighbouring cove
Where oystercatchers and hawks flew and far
Far below in loose heaps small timber lay, tickled
By a thin finger of sea. There I flung the shag,
For in some such place, I thought,
Such bodies best belong, far from bathers, among
The elements that compose and decompose them,
Unconscious, strange to freedom, but perceptible
Through narrow slits that score the skin of things.

Or perhaps (for I could not see the body falling)
A hand rose out of air and plucked the corpse
From its arc and took it, warm still,
To some safer place and concealed it there,
Quite unobtrusively, but sure, but sure.

## *Aesthetics for Benetto Gulgo*

(In memory of Eugen Gottlob Winkler)

OLD men, forgotten, mumbling, all alone,
Must rage with visions, of dark dazzling skin;
Fair Helen's tumbled hair, her body pressed
Under their mouths, but soft, in shared surprise.

Husbands athirst, again, when the great noon
    slackens
Over church and garden, being only half aware
Their fruit is falling, begin to stare and tremble
At wishlike breasts on schoolchildren walking past.

Shall the face that shows no reason for disguise
Make dodderers forfeit wisdom and atone
For sins undone by going fast demented?

Is there such harm in dispossession that we crawl
Backwards through being, mindless, nothing done,
Heart-hollow drab, the whole house unfrequented?

This rose-dissolving wind, this doddering one,
Bequeaths a radiance, absence unconfined.

The line that breasts the form must be like steel,
Dread handling all we have that's beautiful.

## *Alba after Six Years*

THERE was a winter
    dark fell by five
four noses ran
    and shouting children
she got so quickly in a rage

Now when I wake
    through mist and petrol
birdsong cannonades
    blaze open-sighted
at a climbing sun

Hopeful but prone
    I turn to face a wall
between me and that wall
    surprised to meet
wild arms which did not hold this way before.

## *Edward Lear in February*

SINCE last September I've been trying to describe
two moonstone hills,
and an ochre mountain, by candlelight, behind.
But a lizard had been sick into the ink,
a cat keeps clawing at me, you should see my face,
I'm too intent to dodge.

Out of the corner of my eye,
an old man (he's putting almonds into a bag)
stoops in sunlight, closer than the hills.
But all the time these bats flick at me
and plop, like foetuses, all over the blotting paper.
Someone began playing a gong outside, once.

I liked that, it helped; but in a flash
neighbours were pelting him with their slippers and
    things,
bits of coke and old railway timetables.

I have come unstuck in this cellar. Help.
Pacing up and down in my own shadow
has stopped me liking the weight it falls from.
That lizard looks like being sick again. The owls
have built a stinking nest on the Eighteenth Century.

So much for two moonstone hills,
ochre mountain, old man
cramming all those almonds into a bag.

## *The Thousand Things*

DRY vine leaves burn in an angle of the wall.
Dry vine leaves and a sheet of paper, overhung
by the green vine.
From an open grate in an angle of the wall
dry vine leaves and dead flies send smoke up
into the green vine where grape clusters go
ignored by lizards. Dry vine leaves
and a few dead flies on fire
and a Spanish toffee spat
into an angle of the wall,
make a smell that calls to mind
the thousand things. Dead flies go,
paper curls and flares,
Spanish toffee sizzles and the smell
has soon gone over the wall.

A naked child jumps over the threshold,
waving a green spray of leaves of vine.

## CHARLES TOMLINSON

### *Winter Encounters*

HOUSE and hollow; village and valley-side:
The ceaseless pairings; the interchange
In which the properties are constant
Resumes its winter starkness. The hedges' barbs
Are bared. Lengthened shadows
Intersecting, the fields seem parcelled smaller
As if by hedgerow within hedgerow. Meshed
Into neighbourhood by such shifting ties,
The house reposes, squarely upon its acre
Yet with softened angles, the responsive stone
Changeful beneath the changing light:
There is a riding-forth, a voyage impending
In this ruffled air, where all moves
Towards encounter. Inanimate or human,
The distinction fails in these brisk exchanges –
Say, merely, that the roof greets the cloud,
Or by the wall, sheltering its knot of talkers,
Encounter enacts itself in the conversation
On customary subjects, where the mind
May lean at ease, weighing the prospect
Of another's presence. Rain
And the probability of rain, tares
And their progress through a field of wheat –
These, though of moment in themselves,
Serve rather to articulate the sense
That having met, one meets with more
Than the words can witness. One feels behind
Into the intensity that bodies through them
Calmness within the wind, the warmth in cold.

## CHARLES TOMLINSON

### *How Still the Hawk*

How still the hawk
Hangs innocent above
Its native wood:
Distance, that purifies the act
Of all intent, has graced
Intent with beauty.
Beauty must lie
As innocence must harm
Whose end (sited,
Held) is naked
Like the map it cowers on.
And the doom drops:
Plummet of peace
To him who does not share
The nearness and the need,
The shrivelled circle
Of magnetic fear.

### *Poem*

Upended, it crouches on broken limbs
About to run forward. No longer threatened
But surprised into this vigilance
It gapes enmity from its hollowed core.

Moist woodflesh, softened to a paste
Of marl and white splinter, dangles
Where overhead the torn root
Casts up its wounds in a ragged orchis.

The seasons strip, but do not tame you.
I grant you become more smooth
As you are emptied and where the heart shreds
The gap mouths a more practised silence.

You would impress, but merely startle. Your
accomplice
Twilight is dragging its shadows here
Deliberate and unsocial: I leave you
To your one meaning, yourself alone.

## *Farewell to Van Gogh*

THE quiet deepens. You will not persuade
One leaf of the accomplished, steady, darkening
Chestnut-tower to displace itself
With more of violence than the air supplies
When, gathering dusk, the pond brims evenly
And we must be content with stillness.

Unhastening, daylight withdraws from us its shapes
Into their central calm. Stone by stone
Your rhetoric is dispersed until the earth
Becomes once more the earth, the leaves
A sharp partition against cooling blue.

Farewell, and for your instructive frenzy
Gratitude. The world does not end tonight
And the fruit that we shall pick tomorrow
Await us, weighing the unstripped bough.

## *The Churchyard Wall*

STONE against stone, they are building back
Round the steepled bulk, a wall
That enclosed from the neighbouring road
The silent community of graves. James Bridle,
Jonathan Silk and Adam Bliss, you are well housed

Dead, howsoever you lived – such headstones
Lettered and scrolled, and such a wall
To repel the wind. The channel, first,
Dug to contain a base in solid earth
And filled with the weightier fragments. The propped
yews
Will scarcely outlast it; for, breached,
It may be rebuilt. The graves weather
And the stone skulls, more ruinous
Than art had made them, fade by their broken scrolls.
It protects the dead. The living regard it
Once it is falling, and for the rest
Accept it. Again, the ivy
Will clasp it down, save for the buried base
And that, where the frost has cracked,
Must be trimmed, reset, and across its course
The barrier raised. Now they no longer
Prepare: they build, judged by the dead.
The shales must fit, the skins of the wall-face
Flush, but the rising stones
Sloped to the centre, balanced upon an incline.
They work at ease, the shade drawn in
To the uncoped wall which casts it, unmindful
For the moment, that they will be outlasted
By what they create, that their labour
Must be undone. East and west
They cope it edgewise; to the south
Where the talkers sit, taking its sun
When the sun has left it, they have lain
The flat slabs that had fallen inwards
Minded by the ivy. They leave completed
Their intent and useful labours to be ignored,
To pass into common life, a particle
Of the unacknowledged sustenance of the eye,
Less serviceable than a house, but in a world of houses
A merciful structure. The wall awaits decay.

## IAIN CRICHTON SMITH

### *Old Woman*

AND she, being old, fed from a mashed plate
as an old mare might droop across a fence
to the dull pastures of its ignorance.
Her husband held her upright while he prayed

to God who is all-forgiving to send down
some angel somewhere who might land perhaps
in his foreign wings among the gradual crops.
She munched, half dead, blindly searching the spoon.

Outside, the grass was raging. There I sat
imprisoned in my pity and my shame
that men and women having suffered time
should sit in such a place, in such a state

and wished to be away, yes, to be far away
with athletes, heroes, Greeks or Roman men
who pushed their bitter spears into a vein
and would not spend an hour with such decay.

'Pray God,' he said, 'we ask you, God,' he said.
The bowed back was quiet. I saw the teeth
tighten their grip around a delicate death.
And nothing moved within the knotted head

but only a few poor veins as one might see
vague wishless seaweed floating on a tide
of all the salty waters where had died
too many waves to mark two more or three.

## IAIN CRICHTON SMITH

### *Sunday Morning Walk*

SUNDAY of wrangling bells – and salt in the air –
I passed the tall black men and their women walking
over the tight-locked streets which were all on fire
with summer ascendant. The seas were talking and talking

as I took my way to the wood where the river ran quiet.
The grass lay windowed in sunlight, the leaves were raging
in furious dying green. The road turned right
round the upstanding castle whose stone unaging

marks how a world remains as I being now
pack of a wandering flesh take holiday strolling
far from the churches' declaiming. Health will allow
riots of naiads and nymphs, so wantonly rolling

with me in leaves in woods, thinking how once
Jove took his pleasure of Leda or – splendid embracing –
god would mate with a goddess – rapid the pounce,
fruitful the hot-thighed meeting, no need for unlacing.

And occupied thus, I came where a dead sheep lay
close to a fence, days gone. The flies were hissing and
buzzing
out of the boiling eyes, wide open as day.
I stood in the sunlight beside it, watching and musing.

Three crows famished yards off. Live sheep grazed far
from the rotting carcass. The jaw, well-shaved, lay slackly
there on the warm quiet grass. The household air
was busy with buzzing like fever. How quickly, how
quickly

The wool was peeled from the back. How still was the
flesh.
How the visiting flies would not knock at the door of the
sockets.

How the hole in the side gaped red, a well-sized gash.
How the clear young lambs grazed in the shade of the
thickets.

And the sun blazed hot on my shoulder. Here was no shade.
But the sheep was quiet, so quiet. There was nothing to
notice
but the grape-bunched flies and the crows. Could a world
have stayed
if I'd taken a stick in my hand and beat off the flies?

They would merely return when I'd gone and busy as
always
inhabit this larder again, no matter how brightly
I struck with my smart sharp stick. All I could praise –
yes, all I could praise – was the sheep lying there so quietly

not knowing not knowing. High summer was raging
around
I stood in my slack clean clothes. The stones were burning.
The flies in the wound continued their occupied sound
as I turned my back on a death of no weeping or mourning.

## *By Ferry to the Island*

We crossed by ferry to the bare island
where sheep and cows stared coldly through the
wind –
the sea behind us with its silver water,
the silent ferryman standing in the stern
clutching his coat about him like old iron.

We landed from the ferry and went inland
past a small church down to the winding shore
where a white seagull fallen from the failing
chill and ancient daylight lay so pure
and softly breasted that it made more dear

the lesser white around us. There we sat
sheltered by a rock beside the sea.
Someone made coffee, someone played the fool
in a high rising voice for two hours.
The sea's language was more grave and harsh.

And one sat there whose dress was white and cool.
The fool sparkled his wit that she might hear
new diamonds turning on her naked finger.
What might the sea think or the dull sheep
lifting its head through heavy Sunday sleep?

And later, going home, a moon rising
at the end of a cart-track, minimum of red,
the wind being dark, imperfect cows staring
out of their half-intelligence, and a plough
lying on its side in the cold, raw

naked twilight, there began to move
slowly, like heavy water, in the heart
the image of the gull and of that dress,
both being white and out of the darkness rising
the moon ahead of us with its rusty ring.

## *Statement by a Responsible Spinster*

It was my own kindness brought me here
to an eventless room, bare of ornament.
This is the threshold charity carried me over.
I live here slowly in a permanent

but clement weather. It will do for ever.
A barren bulb creates my firmament.
A sister cries: 'I might have learned to wear
sardonic jewellery and the lineament

of a fine beauty, fateful and austere.
I might have trained my perilous armament
on the learnèd and ferocious. A lover
would have emerged uniquely from that element.'

I know that for a lie, product of fever.
This is my beginning. Justice meant
that a man or woman who succumbs to fear
should not be married to good merriment.

I inspect justice through a queer air.
Indeed he lacks significant ornament.
Nevertheless he does not laugh or suffer
though, like pity's cruelty, he too is permanent.

And since I was trapped by pity and the clever
duplicities of age, my last emolument
returns, thus late its flat incurious stare
on my ambiguous love, my only monument.

## *For the Unknown Seaman of the 1939–45 War Buried in Iona Churchyard*

ONE would like to be able to write something for them
not for the sake of the writing but because
a man should be named in dying as well as living,
in drowning as well as on death-bed, and because
the brain being brain must try to establish laws.

Yet these events are not amenable
to any discipline that we can impose
and are not in the end even imaginable.
What happened was simply this, bad luck for those
who have lain here twelve years in a changing pose.

These things happen and there's no explaining,
and to call them 'chosen' might abuse a word.
It is better also not to assume a mourning,
moaning stance. These may have well concurred
in whatever suddenly struck them through the absurd

or maybe meaningful. One simply doesn't
know enough, or understand what came
out of the altering weather in a fashioned
descriptive phrase that was common to each name,
or may have surrounded each like a dear frame.

Best not to make much of it and leave these seamen
in the equally altering acre they now have
inherited from strangers though yet human.
They fell from sea to earth from grave to grave
and, griefless now, taught others how to grieve.

## THOM GUNN

### *Carnal Knowledge*

EVEN in bed I pose: desire may grow
More circumstantial and less circumspect
Each night, but an acute girl would suspect
That my self is not like my body, bare.
I wonder if you know, or, knowing, care?
You know I know you know I know you know.

I am not what I seem, believe me, so
For the magnanimous pagan I pretend
Substitute a forked creature as your friend.
When darkness lies without a roll or stir
Flaccid, you want a competent poseur.
I know you know I know you know I know.

Cackle you hen, and answer when I crow.
No need to grope: I'm still playing the same
Comical act inside the tragic game.
Yet things perhaps are simpler: could it be
A mere tear-jerker void of honesty?
You know I know you know I know you know.

Leave me. Within a minute I will stow
Your greedy mouth, but will not yet to grips.
'There is a space between the breast and lips.'
Also a space between the thighs and head,
So great, we might as well not be in bed.
I know you know I know you know I know.

I hardly hoped for happy thoughts, although
In a most happy sleeping time I dreamt
We did not hold each other in contempt.
Then lifting from my lids night's penny weights
I saw that lack of love contaminates.
You know I know you know I know you know.

Abandon me to stammering, and go;
If you have tears, prepare to cry elsewhere –
I know of no emotion we can share,
Your intellectual protests are a bore
And even now I pose, so now go, for
I know you know.

## *The Wound*

THE huge wound in my head began to heal
About the beginning of the seventh week.
Its valleys darkened, its villages became still:
For joy I did not move and dared not speak,
Not doctors would cure it, but time, its patient skill

And constantly my mind returned to Troy.
After I sailed the seas I fought in turn
On both sides, sharing even Helen's joy
Of place, and growing up – to see Troy burn –
As Neoptolemus, that stubborn boy.

I lay and rested as prescription said.
Manoeuvred with the Greeks, or sallied out
Each day with Hector. Finally my bed
Became Achilles' tent, to which the lout
Thersites came reporting numbers dead.

I was myself: subject to no man's breath:
My own commander was my enemy.
And while my belt hung up, sword in the sheath,
Thersites shambled in and breathlessly
Cackled about my friend Patroclus' death.

I called for armour, rose, and did not reel.
But, when I thought, rage at his noble pain
Flew to my head, and turning I could feel
My wound break open wide. Over again
I had to let those storm-lit valleys heal.

## *Lofty in the Palais de Danse*

YOU are not random picked. I tell you you
Are much like one I knew before, that died.
Shall we sit down, and drink and munch a while
– I want to see if you will really do:
If not we'll get it over now outside.
Wary I wait for one unusual smile.

I never felt this restiveness with her:
I lay calm wanting nothing but what I had.
And now I stand each night outside the Mills
For girls, then shift them to the cinema
Or dance hall . . . Like the world, I've gone to bad.
A deadly world: for, once I like, it kills.

The same with everything: the only posting
I ever liked, was short. And so in me
I kill the easy things that others like
To teach them that no liking can be lasting:
All that you praise I take, what modesty
What gentleness, you ruin while you speak.

And partly that I couldn't if I would
Be bed-content with likenesses so dumb.
Passed in the street, they seem identical
To her original, yet understood
Exhaustively as soon as slept with, some
Lack this, some that, and none like her at all.

You praise my strength. The muscle on my arm.
Yes. Now the other. Yes, about the same.
I've got another muscle you can feel.
Dare say you knew. Only expected harm
Falls from a khaki man. That's why you came
With me and when I go you follow still.

Now that we sway here in the shadowed street
Why can't I keep my mind clenched on the job?
Your body is a good one, not without
Earlier performance, but in this repeat
The pictures are unwilled that I see bob
Out of the dark, and you can't turn them out.

## *Helen's Rape*

HERS was the last authentic rape:
From forced content of common breeder
Bringing the violent dreamed escape
Which came to her in different shape
Than to Europa, Danae, Leda:

Paris. He was a man. And yet
That Aphrodite brought this want
Found too implausible to admit:
And so against this story set
The story of a stolen aunt.

Trust man to prevaricate and disguise
A real event when it takes place:
And Romans stifling Sabine cries
To multiply and vulgarize
What even Trojan did with grace.

Helen herself could not through flesh
Abandon flesh; she felt surround
Her absent body, never fresh
The mortal context, and the mesh
Of the continual battle's sound.

## *The Secret Sharer*

OVER the ankles in snow and numb past pain
I stared up at my window three stories high:

From a white street unconcerned as a dead eye,
I patiently called my name again and again.

The curtains were lit, through glass were lit by doubt
And there was I, within the room alone.
In the empty wind I stood and shouted on:
But O, what if the strange head should peer out?

Suspended taut between two equal fears
I was like to be torn apart by their strong pull:
What, I asked, if I never hear my call?
And what if it reaches my insensitive ears?

Fixed in my socket of thought I saw them move
Aside, I saw that some uncertain hand
Had touched the curtains. Mine, I wondered? And,
At this instant, the wind turned in its groove.

The wind turns in its groove and I am here
Lying in bed, the snow and street outside;
Fire-glow still reassuring; dark defied.
The wind turns in its groove: I am still there.

## *A Mirror for Poets*

It was a violent time. Wheels, racks and fires
In every writer's mouth, and not mere rant.
Certain shrewd herdsmen, between twisted wires
Of penalty folding the realm, were thanked
For organizing spies and secret police
By richness in the flock, which they could fleece.

Hacks in the Fleet and nobles in the Tower
Shakespeare must keep the peace, and Jonson's
    thumb
Be branded (for manslaughter), in the power
Of irons lay the admired Southampton.

Above all swayed the diseased and doubtful queen:
Her state canopied by the glamour of pain.

In this society the boundaries met
Of living, danger, death, leaving no space
Between, except where might be set
That mathematical point whose time and place
Could not exist. Yet at this point they found
Arcadia, a fruitful permanent land.

The faint and stumbling crowds were dim to sight
Who had no time for pity or for terror:
Here moved the Forms, flooding like moonlight
In which might act or thought perceive its error.
The dirty details, calmed and relevant.
Here mankind could behold its whole extent.

Here in a cave the Paphlagonian King
Crouched, waiting for his greater counterpart
Who one remove from likelihood may seem
But several nearer to the human heart.
In exile from dimension, change by storm
Here his huge magnanimity was born.

Yet the historians tell us, life meant less.
It was a violent time, and evil-smelling.
Jonson howled 'Hell's a grammar-school to this.'
But found renunciation well worth telling.
Winnowing with his flail of comedy
He showed coherence in society.

In street, in tavern, happening would cry
'I am myself, but part of something greater,
Find poets what that is, do not pass by
For feel my fingers in your pia mater.
I am a cruelly insistent friend
You cannot smile at me and make an end.'

## *On the Move*

'Man you gotta Go'

THE blue jay scuffling in the bushes follows
Some hidden purpose, and the gust of birds
That spurts across the field, the wheeling swallows,
Have nested in the trees and undergrowth.
Seeking their instinct, or their poise, or both,
One moves with an uncertain violence
Under the dust thrown by a baffled sense
Or the dull thunder of approximate words.

On motorcycles, up the road, they come:
Small, black, as flies hanging in heat, the Boys,
Until the distance throws them forth, their hum
Bulges to thunder held by calf and thigh.
In goggles, donned impersonality,
In gleaming jackets trophied with the dust,
They strap in doubt – by hiding it, robust –
And almost hear a meaning in their noise.

Exact conclusion of their hardiness
Has no shape yet, but from known whereabouts
They ride, direction where the tyres press.
They scare a flight of birds across the field:
Much that is natural, to the will must yield.
Men manufacture both machine and soul,
And use what they imperfectly control
To dare a future from the taken routes.

It is a part solution, after all.
One is not necessarily discord
On earth; or damned because, half animal,
One lacks direct instinct, because one wakes
Afloat on movement that divides and breaks.
One joins the movement in a valueless world,
Choosing it, till, both hurler and the hurled,
One moves as well, always toward, toward.

A minute holds them, who have come to go:
The self-defined, astride the created will
They burst away; the towns they travel through
Are home for neither bird nor holiness,
For birds and saints complete their purposes.
At worst, one is in motion; and at best,
Reaching no absolute, in which to rest,
One is always nearer by not keeping still.

## *Lines for a Book*

I THINK of all the toughs through history
And thank heaven they lived, continually.
I praise the overdogs from Alexander
To those who would not play with Stephen Spender.
Their pride exalted some, some overthrew,
But was not vanity at last: they knew
That though the mind has also got a place
It's not in marvelling at its mirrored face
And evident sensibility. It's better
To go and see your friend than write a letter;
To be a soldier than to be a cripple;
To take an early weaning from the nipple
Than think your mother is the only girl;
To be insensitive, to steel the will,
Than sit irresolute all day at stool
Inside the heart; and to despise the fool,
Who may not help himself and may not choose,
Than give him pity which he cannot use.
I think of those exclusive by their action,
For whom mere thought could be no satisfaction –
The athletes lying under tons of dirt
Or standing gelded so they cannot hurt
The pale curators and the families
By calling up disturbing images.
I think of all the toughs through history
And thank heaven they lived, continually.

## *Elvis Presley*

TWO minutes long it pitches through some bar:
Unreeling from a corner box, the sigh
Of this one, in his gangling finery
And crawling sideburns, wielding a guitar.

The limitations where he found success
Are ground on which he, panting, stretches out
In turn, promiscuously, by every note.
Our idiosyncrasy and likeness.

We keep ourselves in touch with a mere dime:
Distorting hackneyed words in hackneyed songs
He turns revolt into a style, prolongs
The impulse to a habit of the time.

Whether he poses or is real, no cat
Bothers to say: the pose held is a stance,
Which, generation of the very chance
It wars on, may be posture for combat.

## *The Allegory of the Wolf Boy*

THE causes are in Time; only their issue
Is bodied in the flesh, the finite powers.
And how to guess he hides in that firm tissue
Seeds of division? At tennis and at tea
Upon the gentle lawn, he is not ours,
But plays us in a sad duplicity.

Tonight the boy, still boy open and blond,
Breaks from the house, wedges his clothes between
Two moulded garden urns, and goes beyond
His understanding, through the dark and dust:
Fields of sharp stubble, abandoned by machine
To the whirring enmity of insect lust.

As yet ungolden in the dense, hot night
The spikes enter his feet: he seeks the moon,
Which, with the touch of its infertile light,
Shall loose desires hoarded against his will
By the long urging of the afternoon.
Slowly the hard rim shifts above the hill.

White in the beam he stops, faces it square,
And the same instant leaping from the ground
Feels the familiar itch of close dark hair;
Then, clean exception to the natural laws,
Only to instinct and the moon being bound,
Drops on four feet. Yet he has bleeding paws.

## *Jesus and his Mother*

My only son, more God's than mine,
Stay in this garden ripe with pears.
The yielding of their substance wears
A modest and contented shine:
And when they weep with age, not brine
But lazy syrup are their tears.
'I am my own and not my own.'

He seemed much like another man,
That silent foreigner who trod
Outside my door with lily rod:
How could I know what I began
Meeting the eyes more furious than
The eyes of Joseph, those of God?
I was my own and not my own.

And who are these twelve labouring men?
I do not understand your words:

I taught you speech, we named the birds,
You marked their big migrations then
Like any child. So turn again
To silence from the place of crowds.
'I am my own and not my own.'

Why are you sullen when I speak?
Here are your tools, the saw and knife
And hammer on your bench. Your life
Is measured here in week and week
Planed as the furniture you make,
And I will teach you like a wife
To be my own and all my own.

Who like an arrogant wind blown
Where he may please, needs no content?
Yet I remember how you went
To speak with scholars in furred gown.
I hear an outcry in the town;
Who carries that dark instrument?
'One all his own and not his own.'

Treading the green and nimble sward
I stare at a strange shadow thrown.
Are you the boy I bore alone
No doctor near to cut the cord?
I cannot reach to call you Lord,
Answer me as my only son.
'I am my own and not my own.'

## *The Separation*

MUST we for ever eye through space? and make
Contact too much for comfort and yet less,
Like Peter Quint and that strange governess
Divided by a window or a lake?
Deprived like ghost, like man, both glare, then move

Apart in shadow. Must the breath swim between,
The trampled meadow of words yet intervene,
To part desire from the tall muscle of love?
I thought, that night, the evening of the tower,
When I could almost touch you, you were so clear,
That I was Quint and it was all the rest
Kept you away, the children or the hour;

But now you prowl in the garden and I am here,
What dead charge do I pull upon my breast?

## *The Monster*

I LEFT my room at last, I walked
The streets of that decaying town,
I took the turn I had renounced
Where the carved cherub crumbled down.

Eager as to a granted wish
I hurried to the cul-de-sac.
Forestalled by whom? Before the house
I saw an unmoved waiting back.

How had she never vainly mentioned
This lover, too, unsatisfied?
Did she dismiss one every night?
I walked up slowly to his side.

Those eyes glazed like her windowpane,
That wide mouth ugly with despair,
Those arms held tight against the haunches,
Poised, but heavily staying there:

At once I knew him, gloating over
A grief defined and realized,
And living only for its sake.
It was myself I recognized.

I could not watch her window now,
Standing before this man of mine,
The constant one I had created
Lest the pure feeling should decline.

What if I were within the house,
Happier than the fact had been
– Would he, then, still be gazing here,
The man who never can get in?

Or would I, leaving at the dawn
A suppler love than he could guess,
Find him awake on my small bed,
Demanding still some bitterness?

## *The Feel of Hands*

THE hands explore tentatively,
two small live entities whose shapes
I have to guess at. They touch me
all, with the light of fingertips

testing each surface of each thing
found, timid as kittens with it.
I connect them with amusing
hands I have shaken by daylight.

There is a sudden transition:
they plunge together in a full
formed single fury; they are grown
to cats, hunting without scruple;

They are expert but desperate.
I am in the dark. I wonder
when they grew up. It strikes me that
I do not know whose hands they are.

THOM GUNN

## *Black Jackets*

In the silence that prolongs the span
Rawly of music when the record ends,
The red-haired boy who drove a van
In weekday overalls but, like his friends,

Wore cycle boots and jacket here
To suit the Sunday hangout he was in,
Heard, as he stretched back from his beer,
Leather creak softly round his neck and chin.

Before him, on a coal-black sleeve
Remote exertion had lined, scratched, and burned
Insignia that could not revive
The heroic fall or climb where they were earned.

On the other drinkers bent together,
Concocting selves for their impervious kit,
He saw it as no more than leather
Which, taut across the shoulders grown to it,

Sent through the dimness of a bar
As sudden and anonymous hints of light
As those that shipping give, that are
Now flickers on the Bay, now lost in night.

He stretched out like a cat, and rolled
The bitterish taste of beer upon his tongue,
And listened to a joke being told:
The present was the things he stayed among.

If it was only loss he wore,
He wore it to assert, with fierce devotion,
Complicity and nothing more.
He recollected his initiation,

And one especially of the rites.
For on his shoulders they had put tattoos:
The group's name on the left, The Knights,
And on the right the slogan Born To Lose.

## *From the Highest Camp*

NOTHING in this bright region melts or shifts.
The local names are concepts: the Ravine,
Pemmican Ridge, North Col, Death Camp, they mean
The streetless rise, the dazzling abstract drifts,
To which particular names adhere by chance,
From custom lightly, not from character.
We stand on a white terrace and confer;
This is the last camp of experience.

What is that sudden yelp upon the air?
And whose are these cold droppings? whose malformed
Purposeless tracks about the slope? We know.
The abominable endures, existing where
Nothing else can: it is – unfed, unwarmed –
Born of rejection, of the boundless snow.

## *Modes of Pleasure*

I JUMP with terror seeing him,
Dredging the bar with that stiff glare
As fiercely as if each whim there
Were passion, whose passion is a whim:

The Fallen Rake, being fallen from
The heights of twenty to middle age,
And helpless to control his rage,
So mean, so few the chances come.

The very beauty of his prime
Was that the triumphs which recurred
In different rooms without a word
Would all be lost some time in time.

Thus he reduced the wild unknown.
And having used each hour of leisure
To learn by rote the modes of pleasure,
The sensual skills as skills alone,

He knows that nothing, not the most
Cunning or sweet, can hold him still.
Living by habit of the will,
He cannot contemplate the past,

Cannot discriminate, condemned
To the sharpest passion of them all.
Rigid he sits: brave, terrible,
The will awaits its gradual end.

## PETER PORTER

### *Sydney Cove, 1788*

THE Governor loves to go mapping – round and
 round
The inlets of the Harbour in his pinnace.
He fingers a tree-fern, sniffs the ground

And hymns it with a unison of feet –
We march to church and executions. No one,
Even Banks, could match the flora of our fleet.

Grog from Madeira reminds us most of home,
More than the pork and British weevils do.
On a diet of flour, your hair comes out in your comb.

A seaman who tried to lie with a native girl
Ran off when he smelt her fatty hide.
Some say these oysters are the sort for pearls.

Green shoots of the Governor's wheat have browned.
A box of bibles was washed up today,
The chaplain gave them to two methodists. Ross
 found

A convict selling a baby for a jug of rum.
Those black hills which wrestle with
The rain are called Blue Mountains. Come

Genocide or Jesus we can't work this land.
The sun has framed it for our moralists
To dry the bones of forgers in the sand.

We wake in the oven of its cloudless sky,
Already the blood-encircled sun is up.
Mad sharks swim in the convenient sea.

The Governor says we mustn't land a man
Or woman with gonorrhoea. Sound felons only
May leave their bodies in a hangman's land.

Where all is novel, the only rule's explore.
Amelia Levy and Elizabeth Fowles spent the night
With Corporal Plowman and Corporal Winxstead
  for

A shirt apiece. These are our home concerns.
The cantor curlew sings the surf asleep.
The moon inducts the lovers in the ferns.

## *Beast and the Beauty*

His fear never loud in daylight, risen to a night whisper
Of a dead mother in the weatherboard house,
He had this great piece of luck: a girl
In Paris clothes, ex-school monitor, chose
Him for her lover. Twenty-one and experienced,
She showed his hands the presentiment of clothes
And first at a party kissed him, then took
Him home where they did what he'd always supposed.

Her sophistication was his great delight:
Her mother and father drinking, throwing things,
The unhappy marriage, the tradespeople on Christian
Name terms – all the democratic sexiness – mornings
With the Pick of the Pops and the Daily Express
And yet the sudden itching despair, the wonder in King's
College Chapel, the depth that lived in her soul
Of which this raciness was only the worldly covering.

But the sophistication chose to kill – the itch
Was on the inside of the skin. Her family of drunks
Were shrewd, wine-wise young barristers and gentlemen-
Farmers fought for her hand. In the loft there waited trunks
Of heirlooms to be taken seriously. He found himself
Ditched, his calls unanswered, his world shrunk
To eating in Lyons', waiting outside her house at midnight,
Her serious tears to haunt him, boiling on his bunk.

So he sits alone in Libraries, hideous and hairy of soul,
A beast again, waiting for a lustful kiss to bring
Back his human smell, the taste of woman on his tongue.

## *John Marston Advises Anger*

ALL the boys are howling to take the girls to bed.
Our betters say it's a seedy world. The critics say
Think of them as an Elizabethan Chelsea set.
Then they've never listened to our lot – no talk
Could be less like – but the bodies are the same:
Those jeans and bums and sweaters of the King's Road
Would fit Marston's stage. What's in a name,
If Cheapside and the Marshalsea mean Eng. Lit.
And the Fantasie, Sa Tortuga, Grisbi, Bongi-Bo
Mean life? A cliché? What hurts dies on paper,
Fades to classic pain. Love goes as the M.G. goes.
The colonel's daughter in black stockings, hair
Like sash cords, face iced white, studies art,
Goes home once a month. She won't marry the men
She sleeps with, she'll revert to type – it's part
Of the side-show: Mummy and Daddy in the wings,
The bongos fading on the road to Haslemere
Where the inheritors are inheriting still.
Marston's Malheureux found his whore too dear;
Today some Jazz Club girl on the social make
Would put him through his paces, the aphrodisiac cruel.
His friends would be the smoothies of our Elizabethan age –
The Rally Men, Grantchester Breakfast Men, Public School
Personal Assistants and the fragrant P.R.O.s,
Cavalry-twilled tame publishers praising Logue,
Classics Honours Men promoting Jazzetry,
Market Researchers married into Vogue.
It's a Condé Nast world and so Marston's was.
His had a real gibbet – our death's out of sight.

The same thin richness of these worlds remains –
The flesh-packed jeans, the car-stung appetite
Volley on his stage, the cage of discontent.

## *Made in Heaven*

FROM Heals and Harrods come her lovely bridegrooms
(One cheque alone furnished two bedrooms),

From a pantechnicon in the dog-paraded street
Under the orange plane leaves, on workmen's feet

Crunching over Autumn, the fruits of marriage brought
Craftsmen-felt wood, Swedish dressers, a court

Stool tastefully imitated and the wide bed –
(the girl who married money kept her maiden head).

As things were ticked off the Harrods list, there grew
A middle-class maze to pick your way through –

The labour-saving kitchen to match the labour-saving thing
She'd fitted before marriage (O Love, with this ring

I thee wed) – lastly the stereophonic radiogram
And her Aunt's sly letter promising a pram.

Settled in now, the Italian honeymoon over,
As the relatives said, she was living in clover.

The discontented drinking of a few weeks stopped,
She woke up one morning to her husband's alarm-clock,

Saw the shining faces of the wedding gifts from the bed,
Foresaw the cosy routine of the massive years ahead.

As she watched her husband knot his tie for the city,
She thought: I wanted to be a dancer once – it's a pity

I've done none of the things I thought I wanted to,
Found nothing more exacting than my own looks, got
through

Half a dozen lovers whose faces I can't quite remember
(I can still start the Rose Adagio, one foot on the fender)

But at least I'm safe from everything but cancer –
The apotheosis of the young wife and mediocre dancer.

## *Annotations of Auschwitz*

I

WHEN the burnt flesh is finally at rest,
The fires in the asylum grates will come up
And wicks turn down to darkness in the madman's eyes.

II

My suit is hairy, my carpet smells of death,
My toothbrush handle grows a cuticle.
I have six million foulnesses of breath.
Am I mad? The doctor holds my testicles
While the room fills with the zyklon B I cough.

III

On Piccadilly underground I fall asleep –
I shuffle with the naked to the steel door,
Now I am only ten from the front – I wake up –
We are past Gloucester Rd, I am not a Jew,
But scratches web the ceiling of the train.

IV

Around staring buildings the pale flowers grow;
The frenetic butterfly, the bee made free by work,
Rouse and rape the pollen pads, the nectar stoops.
The rusting railway ends here. The blind end in Europe's
gut.

Touch one piece of unstrung barbed wire –
Let it taste blood: let one man scream in pain,
Death's Botanical Gardens can flower again.

V

A man eating his dressing in the hospital
Is lied to by his stomach. It's a final feast to him
Of beef, blood pudding and black bread.
The orderly can't bear to see this mimic face
With its prim accusing picture after death.
On the stiff square a thousand bodies
Dig up useless ground – he hates them all,
These lives ignoble as ungoverned glands.
They fatten in statistics everywhere
And with their sick, unkillable fear of death
They crowd out peace from executioners' sleep.

VI

Forty thousand bald men drowning in a stream –
The like of light on all those bobbing skulls
Has never been seen before. Such death, says the painter,
Is worthwhile – it makes a colour never known.
It makes a sight that's unimagined, says the poet.
It's nothing to do with me, says the man who hates
The poet and the painter. Six million deaths can hardly
Occur at once. What do they make? Perhaps
An idiot's normalcy. I need never feel afraid
When I salt the puny snail – cruelty's grown up
And waits for time and men to bring into its hands
The snail's adagio and all the taunting life
Which has not cared about or guessed its tortured scope.

VII

London is full of chickens on electric spits,
    Cooking in windows where the public pass.
This, say the chickens, is their Auschwitz,
    And all poultry eaters are psychopaths.

## TED HUGHES

### *Famous Poet*

STARE at the monster: remark
How difficult it is to define just what
Amounts to monstrosity in that
Very ordinary appearance. Neither thin nor fat,
Hair between light and dark,

And the general air
Of an apprentice – say, an apprentice house-
Painter amid an assembly of famous
Architects: the demeanour is of mouse,
Yet is he monster.

First scrutinize those eyes
For the spark, the effulgence: nothing. Nothing
there
But the haggard stony exhaustion of a near-
Finished variety artist. He slumps in his chair
Like a badly hurt man, half life-size.

Is it his dreg-boozed inner demon
Still tankarding from tissue and follicle
The vital fire, the spirit electrical
That puts the gloss on a normal hearty male?
Or is it women?

The truth – bring it on
With black drapery, drums, and funeral tread
Like a great man's coffin – no, no, he is not dead
But in this truth surely half-buried:
Once, the humiliation

Of youth and obscurity,
The autoclave of heady ambition trapped,
The fermenting of a yeasty heart stopped –
Burst with such pyrotechnics the dull world gaped
And 'Repeat that!' still they cry.

But all his efforts to concoct
The old heroic bang from their money and praise,
From the parent's pointing finger and the child's
amaze,
Even from the burning of his wreathed bays,
Have left him wrecked: wrecked,

And monstrous, so,
As a Stegosaurus, a lumbering obsolete
Arsenal of gigantic horn and plate
From a time when half the world still burned, set
To blink behind bars at the zoo.

## *Wind*

THIS house has been far out at sea all night,
The woods crashing through darkness, the booming hills,
Winds stampeding the fields under the window
Floundering black astride and blinding wet

Till day rose; then under an orange sky
The hills had new places, and wind wielded
Blade-like, luminous black and emerald,
Flexing like the lens of a mad eye.

At noon I scaled along the house-side as far as
The coal-house door. I dared once to look up –
Through the brunt wind that dented the balls of my eyes
The tent of the hills drummed and strained its guyrope,

The fields quivering, the skyline a grimace,
At any second to bang and vanish with a flap:
The wind flung a magpie away and a black-
Back gull bent like an iron bar slowly. The house

Rang like some fine green goblet in the note
That any second would shatter it. Now deep
In chairs, in front of the great fire, we grip
Our hearts and cannot entertain book, thought,

Or each other. We watch the fire blazing,
And feel the roots of the house move, but sit on,
Seeing the window tremble to come in,
Hearing the stones cry out under the horizons.

## *October Dawn*

OCTOBER is marigold, and yet
A glass half full of wine left out

To the dark heaven all night, by dawn
Has dreamed a premonition

Of ice across its eye as if
The ice-age had begun its heave.

The lawn overtrodden and strewn
From the night before, and the whistling green

Shrubbery are doomed. Ice
Has got its spearhead into place.

First a skin, delicately here
Restraining a ripple from the air,

Soon plate and rivet on pond and brook;
Then tons of chain and massive lock

To hold rivers. Then, sound by sight
Will Mammoth and Sabre-toothed celebrate

Reunion while a fist of cold
Squeezes the fire at the core of the world,

Squeezes the fire at the core of the heart,
And now it is about to start.

## *Vampire*

YOU hosts are almost glad he gate-crashed: see,
How his eyes brighten on the whisky, how his wit
Tumbles the company like a lightning stroke –
You marvel where he gets his energy from . . .

But that same instant, here, far underground,
This fusty carcass stirs its shroud and swells.

'Stop, stop, oh for God's sake, stop!' you shriek
As your tears run down, but he goes on and on
Mercilessly till you think your ribs must crack . . .

While this carcass's eyes grimace, stitched
In the cramp of an ordeal, and a squeeze of blood
Crawls like scorpions into its hair.

You plead, limp, dangling in his mad voice, till
With a sudden blood-spittling cough, he chokes: he
    leaves
Trembling, soon after. You slump back down in a
    chair
Cold as a leaf, your heart scarcely moving . . .

Deep under the city's deepest stone
This grinning sack is bursting with your blood.

## *February*

THE wolf with its belly stitched full of big pebbles;
Nibelung wolves barbed like black pine forest
Against a red sky, over blue snow; or that long grin
Above the tucked coverlet – none suffice.

A photograph; the hairless, knuckled feet
Of the last wolf killed in Britain spoiled him for
wolves:
The worst since has been so much mere Alsatian.
Now it is the dream cries 'Wolf!' where these feet

Print the moonlit doorstep, or run and run
Through the hush of parkland, bodiless, headless;
With small seeming of inconvenience
By day, too, pursue, siege all thought;

Bring him to an abrupt poring stop
Over engravings of gibbet-hung wolves,
As at a cage where the scraggy Spanish wolf
Danced, smiling, brown eyes doggily begging

A ball to be thrown. These feet, deprived,
Disdaining all that are caged, or storied, or pictured,
Through and throughout the true world search
For their vanished head, for the world

Vanished with the head, the teeth, the quick eyes –
Now, lest they choose his head,
Under severe moons he sits making
Wolf-masks, mouths clamped well onto the world.

## *A Woman Unconscious*

RUSSIA and America circle each other;
Threats nudge an act that were without doubt
A melting of the mould in the mother,
Stones melting about the root.

The quick of the earth burned out:
The toil of all our ages a loss
With leaf and insect. Yet flitting thought
(Not to be thought ridiculous)

Shies from the world-cancelling black
Of its playing shadow: it has learned
That there's no trusting (trusting to luck)
Dates when the world's due to be burned;

That the future's no calamitous change
But a malingering of now,
Histories, towns, faces that no
Malice or accident much derange.

And though bomb be matched against bomb,
Though all mankind wince out and nothing
    endure –
Earth gone in an instant flare –
Did a lesser death come

Onto the white hospital bed
Where one, numb beyond her last of sense,
Closed her eyes on the world's evidence
And into pillows sunk her head.

## *Esther's Tomcat*

DAYLONG this tomcat lies stretched flat
As an old rough mat, no mouth and no eyes.
Continual wars and wives are what
Have tattered his ears and battered his head.

Like a bundle of old rope and iron
Sleeps till blue dusk. Then reappear
His eyes, green as ringstones: he yawns wide red,
Fangs fine as a lady's needle and bright.

A tomcat sprang at a mounted knight,
Locked round his neck like a trap of hooks
While the knight rode fighting its clawing and
    bite.
After hundreds of years the stain's there

On the stone where he fell, dead of the tom:
That was at Barnborough. The tomcat still
Grallochs odd dogs on the quiet,
Will take the head clean off your simple pullet,

Is unkillable. From the dog's fury,
From gunshot fired point-blank he brings
His skin whole, and whole
From owlish moons of bekittenings

Among ashcans. He leaps and lightly
Walks upon sleep, his mind on the moon
Nightly over the round world of men
Over the roofs go his eyes and outcry.

## TED HUGHES

# *Hawk Roosting*

I SIT in the top of the wood, my eyes closed.
Inaction, no falsifying dream
Between my hooked head and hooked feet:
Or in sleep rehearse perfect kills and eat.

The convenience of the high trees!
The air's buoyancy and the sun's ray
Are of advantage to me;
And the earth's face upward for my inspection.

My feet are locked upon the rough bark.
It took the whole of Creation
To produce my foot, my each feather:
Now I hold Creation in my foot

Or fly up, and revolve it all slowly –
I kill where I please because it is all mine.
There is no sophistry in my body:
My manners are tearing off heads –

The allotment of death.
For the one path of my flight is direct
Through the bones of the living.
No arguments assert my right:

The sun is behind me.
Nothing has changed since I began.
My eye has permitted no change.
I am going to keep things like this.

## *To Paint a Water Lily*

A GREEN level of lily leaves
Roofs the pond's chamber and paves

The flies' furious arena: study
These, the two minds of this lady.

First observe the air's dragonfly
That eats meat, that bullets by

Or stands in space to take aim;
Others as dangerous comb the hum

Under the trees. There are battle-shouts
And death-cries everywhere hereabouts

But inaudible, so the eyes praise
To see the colours of these flies

Rainbow their arcs, spark, or settle
Cooling like beads of molten metal

Through the spectrum. Think what worse
Is the pond-bed's matter of course;

Prehistoric bedragonned times
Crawl that darkness with Latin names,

Have evolved no improvements there,
Jaws for heads, the set stare,

Ignorant of age as of hour –
Now paint the long-necked lily-flower

Which, deep in both worlds, can be still
As a painting, trembling hardly at all

Though the dragonfly alight,
Whatever horror nudge her root.

## *The Bull Moses*

A HOIST up and I could lean over
The upper edge of the high half-door,
My left foot ledged on the hinge, and look in at the byre's
Blaze of darkness: a sudden shut-eyed look
Backward into the head.

Blackness is depth
Beyond star. But the warm weight of his breathing,
The ammoniac reek of his litter, the hotly-tongued
Mash of his cud, steamed against me.
Then, slowly, as onto the mind's eye –
The brow like masonry, the deep-keeled neck:
Something come up there onto the brink of the gulf,
Hadn't heard of the world, too deep in itself to be called to,
Stood in sleep. He would swing his muzzle at a fly
But the square of sky where I hung, shouting, waving,
Was nothing to him; nothing of our light
Found any reflection in him.

Each dusk the farmer led him
Down to the pond to drink and smell the air,
And he took no pace but the farmer
Led him to take it, as if he knew nothing
Of the ages and continents of his fathers,
Shut, while he wombed, to a dark shed
And steps between his door and the duckpond;
The weight of the sun and the moon and the world
    hammered
To a ring of brass through his nostrils.

He would raise
His streaming muzzle and look out over the meadows,
But the grasses whispered nothing awake, the fetch
Of the distance drew nothing to momentum
In the locked black of his powers. He came strolling gently
    back,

Paused neither toward the pig-pens on his right,
Nor toward the cow-byres on his left: something
Deliberate in his leisure, some beheld future
Founding in his quiet.

I kept the door wide,
Closed it after him and pushed the bolt.

## *View of a Pig*

THE pig lay on a barrow dead.
It weighed, they said, as much as three men.
Its eyes closed, pink white eyelashes.
Its trotters stuck straight out.

Such weight and thick pink bulk
Set in death seemed not just dead.
It was less than lifeless, further off.
It was like a sack of wheat.

I thumped it without feeling remorse.
One feels guilty insulting the dead,
Walking on graves. But this pig
Did not seem able to accuse.

It was too dead. Just so much
A poundage of lard and pork.
Its last dignity had entirely gone.
It was not a figure of fun.

Too dead now to pity.
To remember its life, din, stronghold
Of earthly pleasure as it had been,
Seemed a false effort, and off the point.

Too deadly factual. Its weight
Oppressed me – how could it be moved?

And the trouble of cutting it up!
The gash in its throat was shocking, but not
pathetic.

Once I ran at a fair in the noise
To catch a greased piglet
That was faster and nimbler than a cat,
Its squeal was the rending of metal.

Pigs must have hot blood, they feel like ovens.
Their bite is worse than a horse's –
They chop a half-moon clean out.
They eat cinders, dead cats.

Distinctions and admirations such
As this one was long finished with.
I stared at it a long time. They were going to
scald it,
Scald it and scour it like a doorstep.

## *An Otter*

### I

UNDERWATER eyes, an eel's
Oil of water body, neither fish nor beast is the otter:
Four-legged yet water-gifted, to outfish fish;
With webbed feet and long ruddering tail
And a round head like an old tomcat.

Brings the legend of himself
From before wars or burials, in spite of hounds and
vermin-poles;
Does not take root like the badger. Wanders, cries;
Gallops along land he no longer belongs to;
Re-enters the water by melting.

Of neither water nor land. Seeking
Some world lost when first he dived, that he cannot come
at since,
Takes his changed body into the holes of lakes;
As if blind, cleaves the stream's push till he licks
The pebbles of the source; from sea

To sea crosses in three nights
Like a king in hiding. Crying to the old shape of the
starlit land,
Over sunken farms where the bats go round,
Without answer. Till light and birdsong come
Walloping up roads with the milk wagon.

II

The hunt's lost him. Pads on mud,
Among sedges, nostrils a surface bead,
The otter remains, hours. The air,
Circling the globe, tainted and necessary,

Mingling tobacco-smoke, hounds and parsley,
Comes carefully to the sunk lungs.
So the self under the eye lies,
Attendant and withdrawn. The otter belongs

In double robbery and concealment –
From water that nourishes and drowns, and from land
That gave him his length and the mouth of the hound.
He keeps fat in the limpid integument

Reflections live on. The heart beats thick,
Big trout muscle out of the dead cold;
Blood is the belly of logic; he will lick
The fishbone bare. And can take stolen hold

On a bitch otter in a field full
Of nervous horses, but linger nowhere.
Yanked above hounds, reverts to nothing at all,
To this long pelt over the back of a chair.

## *Thrushes*

TERRIFYING are the attent sleek thrushes on the lawn,
More coiled steel than living – a poised
Dark deadly eye, those delicate legs
Triggered to stirrings beyond sense – with a start, a
    bounce, a stab
Overtake the instant and drag out some writhing thing.
No indolent procrastinations and no yawning stares,
No sighs or head-scratchings. Nothing but bounce and
    stab
And a ravening second.

Is it their single-mind-sized skulls, or a trained
Body, or genius, or a nestful of brats
Gives their days this bullet and automatic
Purpose? Mozart's brain had it, and the shark's mouth
That hungers down the blood-smell even to a leak of its
    own
Side and devouring of itself: efficiency which
Strikes too streamlined for any doubt to pluck at it
Or obstruction deflect.

With a man it is otherwise. Heroisms on horseback,
Outstripping his desk-diary at a broad desk,
Carving at a tiny ivory ornament
For years: his act worships itself – while for him,
Though he bends to be blent in the prayer, how loud and
    above what
Furious spaces of fire do the distracting devils
Orgy and hosannah, under what wilderness
Of black silent water weep.

## *Pike*

PIKE, three inches long, perfect
Pike in all parts, green tigering the gold.
Killers from the egg: the malevolent aged grin.
They dance on the surface among the flies.

Or move, stunned by their own grandeur,
Over a bed of emerald, silhouette
Of submarine delicacy and horror,
A hundred feet long in their world.

In ponds, under the heat-struck lily pads –
Gloom of their stillness:
Logged on last year's black leaves, watching
    upwards.
Or hung in an amber cavern of weeds.

The jaws' hooked clamp and fangs
Not to be changed at this date;
A life subdued to its instrument;
The gills kneading quietly, and the pectorals.

Three we kept behind glass,
Jungled in weed: three inches, four,
And four and a half: fed fry to them –
Suddenly there were two. Finally one

With a sag belly and the grin it was born with.
And indeed they spare nobody.
Two, six pounds each, over two feet long,
High and dry and dead in the willow-herb –

One jammed past its gills down the other's gullet:
The outside eye stared: as a vice locks –
The same iron in this eye
Though its film shrank in death.

The pond I fished, fifty yards across,
Whose lilies and muscular tench
Had outlasted every visible stone
Of the monastery that planted them –

Stilled legendary depth:
It was as deep as England. It held
Pike too immense to stir, so immense and old
That past nightfall I dared not cast

But silently cast and fished
With the hair frozen on my head
For what might move, for what eye might move.
The still splashes on the dark pond,

Owls hushing the floating woods
Frail on my ear against the dream
Darkness beneath night's darkness had freed,
That rose slowly towards me, watching.

## *Snowdrop*

Now is the globe shrunk tight
Round the mouse's dulled wintering heart.
Weasel and crow, as if moulded in brass,
Move through an outer darkness
Not in their right minds,
With the other deaths. She, too, pursues her ends,
Brutal as the stars of this month,
Her pale head heavy as metal.

## *Sunstroke*

FRIGHTENING the blood in its tunnel
The mowing machine ate at the field of grass.

My eyes had been glared dark. Through a red heat
The cradled guns, damascus, blued, flared –

At every stir sliding their molten embers
Into my head. Sleekly the clover

Bowed and flowed backward
Over the saw-set swimming blades

Till the blades bit – roots, stones, ripped into red –
Some baby's body smoking among the stalks.

Reek of paraffin oil and creosote
Swabbing my lungs doctored me back

Laid on a sack in the great-beamed engine-shed.
I drank at stone, at iron of plough and harrow;

Dulled in a pit, heard thick walls of rain
And voices in swaddled confinement near me

Warm as veins. I lay healing
Under the ragged length of a dog fox

That dangled head downward from one of the beams,
With eyes open, forepaws strained at a leap –

Also surprised by the rain.

## *Gog*

I WOKE to a shout – 'I am Alpha and Omega.'
Rocks and a few trees trembled
Deep in their own country.
I ran and an absence bounded beside me.

The dog's god is a scrap dropped from the table,
The mouse's saviour is a ripe wheat grain.
Hearing the Messiah cry
My mouth widens in adoration.

How fat are the lichens!
They cushion themselves on the silence.
The dust, too, is replete.
The air wants for nothing.

What was my error? My skull has sealed it out.
My great bones are massed in me.
They pound on the earth, my song excites them.
I do not look at the rocks and trees. I am frightened
    of what they see.

I listen to the song jarring my mouth
Where the skull-rooted teeth are in possession.
I am massive on earth. My feetbones beat on the earth,
Over the sounds of motherly weeping....

After I drink at a pool quietly.
The horizons bear the rocks and trees away into
    twilight.
I lie down. I become darkness –
Darkness that all night sings and circles stamping.

## *Pibroch*

THE sea cries with its meaningless voice,
Treating alike its dead and its living,
Probably bored with the appearance of heaven
After so many millions of nights without sleep,
Without purpose, without self-deception.

Stone likewise. A pebble is imprisoned
Like nothing in the Universe.
Created for black sleep. Or growing
Conscious of the sun's red spot occasionally,
Then dreaming it is the foetus of God.

Over the stone rushes the wind
Able to mingle with nothing,
Like the hearing of the blind stone itself.
Or turns, as if the stone's mind came feeling
A fantasy of directions.

Drinking the sea and eating the rock
A tree struggles to make leaves –
An old woman fallen from space
Unprepared for these conditions.
She hangs on, because her mind's gone completely.

Minute after minute, aeon after aeon,
Nothing lets up or develops.
And this is neither a bad variant nor a tryout.
This is where the staring angels go through.
This is where all the stars bow down.

## JON SILKIN

### *Death of a Son*

(who died in a mental hospital aged one)

SOMETHING has ceased to come along with me.
Something like a person: something very like one.
And there was no nobility in it
Or anything like that.

Something was there like a one year
Old house, dumb as stone. While the near buildings
Sang like birds and laughed
Understanding the pact

They were to have with silence. But he
Neither sang nor laughed. He did not bless silence
Like bread, with words.
He did not forsake silence.

But rather, like a house in mourning
Kept the eye turned in to watch the silence while
The other houses like birds
Sang around him.

And the breathing silence neither
Moved nor was still.

I have seen stones: I have seen brick
But this house was made up of neither bricks nor stone
But a house of flesh and blood
With flesh of stone

And bricks for blood. A house
Of stones and blood in breathing silence with the other
Birds singing crazy on its chimneys.
But this was silence,

This was something else, this was
Hearing and speaking though he was a house drawn
Into silence, this was
Something religious in his silence,

Something shining in his quiet,
This was different this was altogether something else:
Though he never spoke, this
Was something to do with death.

And then slowly the eye stopped looking
Inward. The silence rose and became still.
The look turned to the outer place and stopped,
With the birds still shrilling around him.
And as if he could speak

He turned over on his side with his one year
Red as a wound
He turned over as if he could be sorry for this
And out of his eyes two great tears rolled, like stones,
and he died.

## *The Child*

SOMETHING that can be heard
Is a grasping of soft fingers
Behind that door.
Oh come in, please come in
And be seated.

It was hard to be sure,
Because for some time a creature
Had bitten at the wood.
But this was something else; a pure noise
Humanly shaped

That gently insists on
Being present. I am sure you are.
Look: the pots over the fire
On a shelf, just put;
So, and no other way,

Are as you have seen them; and you,
Being visible, make them no different.
No man nor thing shall take
Your place from you; so little,
You would think, to ask for.

I have not denied; you know that.
Do you? Do you see
How you are guttered
At a breath, a flicker from me?
Burn more then.

Move this way with me,
Over the stone. Here are
Your father's utensils on
The kitchen wall; cling
As I lead you.

It seems you have come without speech,
And flesh. If it be love
That moves with smallness tnrough
These rooms, speak to me,
As you move.

You have not come with
Me, but burn on the stone.

If I could pick you up
If I could lift you;
Can a thing be weightless?
I have seen, when I did lift you

How your flesh was casually
Pressed in. You have come
Without bone, or blood.
Is that to be preferred?
A flesh without

Sinew, a bone that has
No hardness, and will not snap.
Hair with no spring; without
Juices, touching, or speech.
What are you?

Or rather, show me, since
You cannot speak, that you are real;
A proper effusion of air,
Not that I doubt, blown by a breath
Into my child;

As if you might grow on that vapour
To thought, or natural movement
That expresses, 'I know where I am.'
Yet that you are here,
I feel.

Though you are different.
The brain being touched lightly,
It was gone. Yet since you live,
As if you were not born,
Strangeness of strangeness, speak.

Or rather, touch my breath
With your breath, steadily
And breathe yourself into me.

The soft huge pulsing comes
And passes through my flesh
Out of my hearing.

## *Lilies of the Valley*

Minute flowers harden. Depend
From thin bowing stem;
Are white as babies' teeth.
With broad leaves, immobile;
Are sheath-like, and fat.
What have these to do with beauty?
They must take you with
A fingering odour, clutches the senses,
Fills the creases and tightens the wind's seams,
As noise does. The plant is equipped.
Even then you don't like it.
Gradually though
Its predatory scent
Betters you, forces you, and more than
The protected rose creating
A sculptured distant adulation
For itself. This insinuates, then grapples you,
Being hungry; not poised, not gerundive.
Hard, and uncrushed, these flowerheads;
Like beads, in your palm.
You cannot destroy that conquering amorousness
Drenches the glands, and starts
The belled memory. Glows there, with odour.
Memorable as the skin
Of a fierce animal.

## *A Daisy*

Look unoriginal
Being numerous. They ask for attention
With that gradated yellow swelling
Of oily stamens. Petals focus them:
The eye-lashes grow wide.

Why should not one bring these to a funeral?
And at night, like children,
Without anxiety, their consciousness
Shut with white petals.

Blithe, individual.

The unwearying, small sunflower
Fills the grass
With versions of one eye.
A strength in the full look
Candid, solid, glad.
Domestic as milk.

In multitudes, wait,
Each, to be looked at, spoken to.
They do not wither;
Their going, a pressure
Of elate sympathy
Released from you.
Rich up to the last interval
With minute tubes of oil, pollen;
Utterly without scent, for the eye,
For the eye, simply. For the mind
And its invisible organ,
That feeling thing.

JON SILKIN

## *Dandelion*

Slugs nestle where the stem
Broken, bleeds milk.
The flower is eyeless: the sight is compelled
By small, coarse, sharp petals,
Like metal shreds. Formed,
They puncture, irregularly perforate
Their yellow, brutal glare.

And certainly want to
Devour the earth. With an ample movement
They are a foot high, as you look.
And coming back, they take hold
On pert domestic strains.
Others' lives are theirs. Between them
And domesticity,
Grass. They infest its weak land;
Fatten, hide slugs, infestate.
They look like plates; more closely
Like the first tryings, the machines, of nature
Riveted into her, successful.

## GEOFFREY HILL

### *Genesis*

I

AGAINST the burly air I strode,
Where the tight ocean heaves its load,
Crying the miracles of God.

And first I brought the sea to bear
Upon the dead weight of the land;
And the waves flourished at my prayer,
The rivers spawned their sand.

And where the streams were salt and full
The tough pig-headed salmon strove,
Curbing the ebb and the tide's pull,
To reach the steady hills above.

II

The second day I stood and saw
The osprey plunge with triggered claw,
Feathering blood along the shore,
To lay the living sinew bare.

And the third day I cried: 'Beware
The soft-voiced owl, the ferret's smile,
The hawk's deliberate stoop in air,
Cold eyes, and bodies hooped in steel,
Forever bent upon the kill.'

III

And I renounced, on the fourth day,
This fierce and unregenerate clay,

Building as a huge myth for man
The watery Leviathan,

And made the glove-winged albatross
Scour the ashes of the sea
Where Capricorn and Zero cross,
A brooding immortality –
Such as the charmed phoenix has
In the unwithering tree.

### IV

The phoenix burns as cold as frost;
And, like a legendary ghost,
The phantom-bird wild and lost,
Upon a pointless ocean toseed.

So, the fifth day, I turned again
To flesh and blood and the blood's pain.

### V

On the sixth day, as I rode
In haste about the works of God,
With spurs I plucked the horse's blood.

By blood we live, the hot, the cold,
To ravage and redeem the world:
There is no bloodless myth will hold.

And by Christ's blood are men made free
Though in close shrouds their bodies lie
Under the rough pelt of the sea;

Though Earth has rolled beneath her weight
The bones that cannot bear the light.

## *God's Little Mountain*

BELOW, the river scrambled like a goat
Dislodging stones. The mountain stamped its foot,
Shaking, as from a trance. And I was shut
With wads of sound into a sudden quiet.

I thought the thunder had unsettled heaven,
All was so still. And yet the sky was cloven
By flame that left the air cold and engraven.
I waited for the word that was not given,

Pent up into a region of pure force,
Made subject to the pressure of the stars;
I saw the angels lifted like pale straws;
I could not stand before those winnowing eyes

And fell, until I found the world again.
Now I lack grace to tell what I have seen;
For though the head frames words the tongue has
none,
And who will prove the surgeon to this stone?

## *Holy Thursday*

NAKED, he climbed to the wolf's lair;
He beheld Eden without fear,
Finding no ambush offered there
But sleep under the harbouring fur.

He said: 'They are decoyed by love
Who, tarrying through the hollow grove,
Neglect the seasons' sad remove.
Child and nurse walk hand in glove

As unaware of Time's betrayal,
Weaving their innocence with guile.
But they must cleave the fire's peril
And suffer innocence to fall.

I have been touched with that fire,
And have fronted the she-wolf's lair.
Lo, she lies gentle and innocent of desire
Who was my constant myth and terror.'

## *Merlin*

I WILL consider the outnumbering dead:
For they are the husks of what was rich seed.
Now, should they come together to be fed,
They would outstrip the locusts' covering tide.

Arthur, Elaine, Mondred; they are all gone
Among the raftered galleries of bone.
By the long barrows of Logres they are made one,
And over their city stands the pinnacled corn.

## *In Memory of Jane Fraser*

WHEN snow like sheep lay in the fold
And winds went begging at each door,
And the far hills were blue with cold,
And a cold shroud lay on the moor,

She kept the siege. And every day
We watched her brooding over death
Like a strong bird above its prey.
The room filled with the kettle's breath.

Damp curtains glued against the pane
Sealed time away. Her body froze

As if to freeze us all, and chain
Creation to a stunned repose.

She died before the world could stir.
In March the ice unloosed the brook
And water ruffled the sun's hair,
And a few sprinkled leaves unshook.

## *The Turtle Dove*

LOVE that drained her drained him she'd loved, though
each
For the other's sake forged passion upon speech,
Bore their close days through sufferance towards night
Where she at length grasped sleep and he lay quiet

As though needing no questions, now, to guess
What her secreting heart could not well hide.
Her caught face flinched in half-sleep at his side.
Yet she, by day, modelled her real distress,

Poised, turned her cheek to the attending world
Of children and intriguers and the old,
Conversed freely, exercised, was admired,
Being strong to dazzle. All this she endured

To affront him. He watched her rough grief work
Under the formed surface of habit. She spoke
Like one long undeceived but she was hurt.
She denied more love, yet her starved eyes caught

His, devouring, at times. Then, as one self-dared,
She went to him, plied there; like a furious dove
Bore down with visitations of such love
As his lithe, fathoming heart absorbed and buried.

## *The Troublesome Reign*

So much he had from fashion and no more:
Her trained hard gaze, brief lips whose laughter spat
Concession to desire – she suffered that,
Feeding a certain green-fuel to his fire.

Reluctant heat! This burning of the dead
Could consume her also; she moved apart
As if, through such denial, he might be made
Himself again familiar and unscarred,

Contained, even wary, though not too much
To take pleasure considering her flesh shone,
Her salt-worn summer dress. But he had gone
Thirty days through such a dream of taste and touch

When the sun stood for him and the violent larks
Stabbed up into the sun. She was his, then,
Her limbs grasped him, satisfied, while his brain
Judged every move and cry from its separate dark.

More dark, more separate, now, yet still not dead,
Their mouths being drawn to public and private
    speech –
Though there was too much care in all he said,
A hard kind of no-feeling in her touch –

By such rites they saved love's face, and such laws
As prescribe mutual tolerance, charity
To neighbours, strangers, those by nature
Subdued among famines and difficult wars.

## *Requiem for the Plantagenet Kings*

For whom the possessed sea littered, on both shores,
Ruinous arms; being fired, and for good,
To sound the constitution of just wars,
Men, in their eloquent fashion, understood.

Relieved of soul, the dropping-back of dust,
Their usage, pride, admitted within doors;
At home, under caved chantries, set in trust,
With well-dressed alabaster and proved spurs
They lie; they lie; secure in the decay
Of blood, blood-marks, crowns hacked and coveted,
Before the scouring fires of trial-day
Alight on men; before sleeked groin, gored head,
Budge through the clay and gravel, and the sea
Across daubed rock evacuates its dead.

## *Canticle for Good Friday*

The cross staggered him. At the cliff-top
Thomas, beneath its burden, stood
While the dulled wood
Spat on the stones each drop
Of deliberate blood.

A clamping, cold-figured day
Thomas (not transfigured) stamped, crouched,
Watched,
Smelt vinegar and blood. He,
As yet unsearched, unscratched,

And suffered to remain
At such near distance
( A slight miracle might cleanse
His brain
Of all attachments, claw-roots of sense)

In unaccountable darkness moved away
The strange flesh untouched, carrion-sustenance
Of staunchest love, choicest defiance,
Creation's issue congealing (and one woman's).

## *In Piam Memoriam*

I

CREATED purely from glass the saint stands,
Exposing his gifted quite empty hands
Like a conjurer about to begin,
A righteous man begging of righteous men.

II

In the sun lily-and-gold-coloured,
Filtering the cruder light, he has endured,
A feature for our regard; and will keep;
Of wordly purity the stained archetype.

III

The scummed pond twitches. The great holly-tree,
Emptied and shut, blows clear of wasting snow,
The common, puddled substance: beneath,
Like a revealed mineral, a new earth.

## GEORGE MACBETH

### *The Return*

AFTER the light has set
First I imagine silence: then the stroke
As if some drum beat outside has come in.
And in the silence I smell moving smoke
And feel the touch of coarse cloth on my skin.
And all is darkness yet
Save where the hot wax withers by my chin.

When I had fallen (bone
Bloodying wet stone) he would lead me back
Along the street and up the corkscrew stair
(Time running anti-clockwise, fingers slack)
And open windows to let in fresh air
And leave me stretched alone
With sunken cheeks drained whiter than my hair.

Then I was young. Before
Another stroke he will come back in bone
And thin my heart. That soot-black hill will break
And raise him in his clay suit from the stone
While my chalk-ridden fingers dryly ache
And burn. On this rush floor
He will come striding hotly. When I wake

The stroke will have been tolled
And I shall take his crushed purse in my hand
And feel it pulse (warm, empty) on my wrist.
Blood floods my temples. Clay man, from what land
Have you come back to keep your freezing tryst
With someone grown so old?
Soldier, forgive me. Candles die in mist

And now a cold wind stirs
Inside the shuttered room. I feel his hand
Brushing the stale air, feeling for my place
Across the phlegm-soaked pillows. I am sand
Threading a glass with slow and even pace
And dying in my furs.
My father turns, with tears on his young face.

## *Mother Superior*

SISTERS, it will be necessary
To prepare a cool retreat. See to
It that several basins are filled
Nightly with fresh water and placed there.
Take care that food for a long stay be

Provided in sealed jars. I know of
No way to protect an outer room
From the light but some must be tried. Let
The walls be made thick to keep out the
Heat. Before the Annunciation

Our Lord exacts no other service.
It may seem prudent to wear a wool
Robe at all times and to bow down when
The Word comes. Remember the parable
Of the Virgins and pray for all the

Unpremeditating. 'The brides of
Our Lord in their burrows' may not be
A flattering title but the known
Future lies in the wombs of prepared
Rabbits. To bear a pure strain with no

Care for the world's corruption requires
Courage, sisters. Creating a safe

Place for the incarnation of what
One can scarcely imagine without
Madness might seem a demeaning task.

In the Order of Resurrection
Of which you are acolytes there is
No more noble service. Remember
The Code. Your duty is not to the
Sick but to the unborn. Perform it.

## *Bedtime Story*

LONG long ago when the world was a wild place
Planted with bushes and peopled by apes, our
Mission Brigade was at work in the jungle.
    Hard by the Congo

Once, when a foraging detail was active
Scouting for green-fly, it came on a grey man, the
Last living man, in the branch of a baobab
    Stalking a monkey.

Earlier men had disposed of, for pleasure,
Creatures whose names we scarcely remember –
Zebra, rhinoceros, elephants, wart-hog,
    Lion, rats, deer. But

After the wars had extinguished the cities
Only the wild ones were left, half-naked
Near the Equator: and here was the last one,
    Starved for a monkey.

By then the Mission Brigade had encountered
Hundreds of such men: and their procedure,
History tells us, was only to feed them:
    Find them and feed them;

Those were the orders. And this was the last one.
Nobody knew that he was, but he was. Mud
Caked on his flat grey flanks. He was crouched, half-armed with a shaved spear

Glinting beneath broad leaves. When their jaws cut
Swathes through the bark and he saw fine teeth shine,
Round eyes roll round and forked arms waver
Huge as the rough trunks

Over his head, he was frightened. Our workers
Marched through the Congo before he was born, but
This was the first time perhaps that he'd seen one.
Staring in hot still

Silence, he crouched there: then jumped. With a long swing
Down from his branch, he had angled his spear too
Quickly, before they could hold him, and hurled it
Hard at the soldier

Leading the detail. How could he know Queen's
Orders were only to help him? The soldier
Winced when the tipped spear pricked him. Unsheathing his
Sting was a reflex.

Later the Queen was informed. There were no more
Men. An impetuous soldier had killed off,
Purely by chance, the penultimate primate.
When she was certain,

Squadrons of workers were fanned through the Congo
Detailed to bring back the man's picked bones to be
Sealed in the archives in amber. I'm quite sure
Nobody found them

After the most industrious search, though.
Where had the bones gone? Over the earth, dear,
Ground by the teeth of the termites, blown by the
Wind, like the dodo's.

## *The God of Love*

'The musk-ox is accustomed to near-Arctic conditions. When danger threatens, these beasts cluster together to form a defensive wall or a "porcupine" with the calves in the middle.'

Dr Wolfgang Engelhardt: *Survival of the Free*

I FOUND them between far hills, by a frozen lake,
On a patch of bare ground. They were grouped
In a solid ring, like an ark of horn. And around
Them circled, slowly closing in,
Their tongues lolling, their ears flattened against the wind,

A whirlpool of wolves. As I breathed, one fragment of bone and
Muscle detached itself from the mass and
Plunged. The pad of the pack slackened, as if
A brooch had been loosened. But when the bull
Returned to the herd, the revolving collar was tighter. And only

The windward owl, uplifted on white wings
In the glass of air, alert for her young,
Soared high enough to look into the cleared centre
And grasp the cause. To the slow brain
Of each beast by the frozen lake what lay in the cradle of their crowned

Heads of horn was a sort of god-head. Its brows
Nudged when the ark was formed. Its need
Was a delicate womb away from the iron collar
Of death, a cave in the ring of horn
Their encircling flesh had backed with fur. That the collar of death

Was the bone of their own skulls: that a softer womb
Would open between far hills in a plunge

Of bunched muscles: and that their immortal calf lay
Dead on the snow with its horns dug into
The ice for grass: they neither saw nor felt. And yet if

That hill of fur could split and run – like a river
Of ice in thaw, like a broken grave –
It would crack across the icy crust of withdrawn
Sustenance and the rigid circle
Of death be shivered: the fed herd would entail its under-fur

On the swell of a soft hill and the future be sown
On grass, I thought. But the herd fell
By the bank of the lake on the plain, and the pack closed,
And the ice remained. And I saw that the god
In their ark of horn was a god of love, who made them die.

## *Owl*

is my favourite. Who flies
like a nothing through the night,
who-whoing. Is a feather
duster in leafy corners ring-a-rosy-ing
boles of mice. Twice

you hear him call. Who
is he looking for? You hear
him hoovering over the floor
of the wood. O would you be gold
rings in the driving skull

if you could? Hooded and
vulnerable by the winter suns

owl looks. Is the grain of bark
in the dark. Round beaks are at
work in the pellety nest,

*picked up pellet*

resting. Owl is an eye
in the barn. For a hole
in the trunk owl's blood
is to blame. Black talons in the
petrified fur! Cold walnut hands

*owl with its strength dug in that hole in another animal —*

*of an animal!*

on the case of the brain! In the reign
of the chicken owl comes like
a god. Is a goad in
the rain to the pink eyes,
dripping. For a meal in the day

*stick used to irritate/annoy*

*owls' activity*

flew, killed, on the moor. Six
mouths are the seed of his
arc in the season. Torn meat
from the sky. Owl lives
by the claws of his brain. On the branch

*baby chicks — His chicks —*

in the sever of the hand's
twigs owl is a backward look.
Flown wind in the skin. Fine
rain in the bones. Owl breaks
like the day. Am an owl, am an owl.

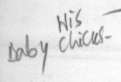

## PETER REDGROVE

### *Lazarus and the Sea*

THE tide of my death came whispering like this
Soiling my body with its tireless voice.
I scented the antique moistures when they sharpened
The air of my room, made the rough wood of my bed,
    (most dear),
Standing out like roots in my tall grave.
They slopped in my mouth and entered my plaited blood
Quietened my jolting breath with a soft argument
Of such measured insistence, untied the great knot of my
    heart.
They spread like whispered conversations
Through all the numbed rippling tissues radiated
Like a tree for thirty years from the still centre
Of my salt ovum. But this calm dissolution
Came after my agreement to the necessity of it;
Where before it was a storm over red fields
Pocked with the rain and the wheat furrowed
With wind, then it was the drifting of smoke
From a fire of the wood, damp with sweat,
Fallen in the storm.

I could say nothing of where I had been,
But I knew the soil in my limbs and the rain-water
In my mouth, knew the ground as a slow sea unstable
Like clouds and tolerating no organization such as mine
In its throat of my grave. The knotted roots
Would have entered my nostrils and held me
By the armpits, woven a blanket for my cold body
Dead in the smell of wet earth, and raised me to the sky
For the sun in the slow dance of the seasons.
Many gods like me would be laid in the ground

Dissolve and be formed again in this pure night
Among the blessing of birds and the sifting water.
But where was the boatman and his gliding punt?
The judgement and the flames? These happenings
Were much spoken of in my childhood and the legends.
And what judgement tore me to life, uprooted me
Back to my old problems and to the family,
Charged me with unfitness for this holy simplicity?

## *Old House*

I LAY in an agony of imagination as the wind
Limped up the stairs and puffed on the landings,
Snuffled through floorboards from the foundations,
Tottered, withdrew into flaws, and shook the house.
Peppery dust swarmed through all cracks,
The boiling air blew a dry spume from other mouths,
From other hides and function:
Scale of dead people fountained to the ceiling –
What sort of a house is this to bring children to,

Burn it down, build with new-fired brick;
How many times has this place been wound up
Around the offensive memories of a dead person,
Or a palette of sick colours dry on the body,
Or bare arms through a dank trapdoor to shut off water,
Or windows filmed over the white faces of children:
'This is no place to bring children to'

I cried in a nightmare of more
Creatures shelled in bone-white,
Or dead eyes fronting soft ermine faces,
Or mantled in carnation, dying kings of creation,
Or crimson mouth-skirts flashing as they pass:
What a world to bring new lives into,

Flat on my back in a warm bed as the house around me
Lived in the wind more than the people that built it;
It was bought with all our earned money,
With all the dust I was nearly flying from my body
That whipped in the wind in this normal November,
And outstretched beside her in my silly agony
She turned in her sleep and called for me,
Then taught me what children were to make a home for.

## *Early Morning Feed*

THE father darts out on the stairs
To listen to that keening
In the upper room, for a change of note
That signifies distress, to scotch disaster,
The kettle humming in the room behind.

He thinks, on tiptoe, ears a-strain,
The cool dawn rising like the moon:
'Must not appear and pick him up;
He mustn't think he has me springing
To his beck and call,'
The kettle rattling behind the kitchen door.

He has him springing
A-quiver on the landing –
For a distress-note, a change of key,
To gallop up the stairs to him
To take him up, light as a violin,
And stroke his back until he smiles.
He sidles in the kitchen
And pours his tea . . .

And again stands hearkening
For milk cracking the lungs.
There's a little panting,

A cough: the thumb's in: he'll sleep,
The cup of tea cooling on the kitchen table.

Can he go in now to his chair and think
Of the miracle of breath, pick up a book,
Ready at all times to take it at a run
And intervene between him and disaster,
Sipping his cold tea as the sun comes up?

He returns to bed
And feels like something, with the door ajar,
Crouched in the bracken, alert, with big eyes
For the hunter, death, disaster.

## *Bedtime Story for my Son*

WHERE did the voice come from? I hunted through the
rooms
For that small boy, that high, that head-voice,
The clatter as his heels caught on the door,
A shadow just caught moving through the door
Something like a school-satchel. My wife
Didn't seem afraid, even when it called for food
She smiled and turned her book and said:
'I couldn't go and love the empty air.'

We went to bed. Our dreams seemed full
Of boys in one or another guise, the paper-boy
Skidding along in grubby jeans, a music-lesson
She went out in the early afternoon to fetch a child from.
I pulled up from a pillow damp with heat
And saw her kissing hers, her legs were folded
Far away from mine. A pillow! It seemed
She couldn't love the empty air.

Perhaps, we thought, a child had come to grief
In some room in the old house we kept,
And listened if the noises came from some especial room,
And then we'd take the boards up and discover
A pile of dusty bones like charcoal twigs and give
The tiny-sounding ghost a proper resting-place
So that it need not wander in the empty air.

No blood-stained attic harboured the floating sounds,
We found they came in rooms that we'd warmed with our
    life.
We traced the voice and found where it mostly came
From just underneath both our skins, and not only
In the night-time either, but at the height of noon
And when we sat at meals alone. Plainly, this is how we
    found
That love pines loudly to go out to where
It need not spend itself on fancy and the empty air.

## *Foundation*

BEHIND her belly like a sleeping eye
Wellington-booted the shock-haired boy
Kicks up puddles like a spattering pen,
Knocks conkers and sprints through under
    leaves,
Watches my toecaps as he tackles a fib.

Behind her belly like a swollen grape
Full of rich waters, a man proposes,
And with a ramrod jerk makes many eyes
And opens them, and causes breath
To whistle through empty unsealed nostrils.

With triple weight we limp upstairs.
Behind her belly, like a schoolroom globe,
Work many peoples, and we guess their name,
Care for their weight as we fetch our own
And should our various neighbours'.

## *The Archaeologist*

So I take one of those thin plates
And fit it to a knuckled other,
Carefully, for it trembles on the edge of powder,
Restore the jaw and find the fangs their mates.

The thorny tree of which this is the gourd,
Outlasting centuries of grit and water,
Re-engineered by me, stands over there,
Stocky, peeling, crouched and dangling-pawed.

I roll the warm wax within my palm
And to the bone slowly mould a face
Of the jutting-jawed, hang-browed race;
On the brute strength I try to build up a calm,

For it is a woman, by the broad hips;
I give her a smooth skin, and make the mouth mild:
It is aeons since she saw her child
Spinning thin winds of gossamer from his lips.

## *The Affianced*

He excites the pebbles like dice clicking under our feet,
He walks on the ocean and it goggles with His sun
Or He sighs, and the waves are a city of doors slamming;
God's arm engloves this tree and brandishes it

His panting lynches whole forests of catkins
His yellow eye roils in that daisy;
He launches the squirrels like fur jets with dry claws
If He uses the mud it rainbows with oils and liquors
If He gets behind the hemlocks they branch acutely
Their foam-head flowers sudden silent amphitheatres
So that my cry of warning pulses unheeded
At the very brink of the spitting cliffs –
And with all these instruments courting his body and spirit
By the glistening of his eyes and broken breathing
There is no need for mine where there is God's touch. . . .

So I stand aside in flared cottons witnessing His power on
 him
Waiting for Him to eat or enter me, so long as I can keep
 my head,
And be the only inspiration of these that to the last shall
 act in kindness.

## *For No Good Reason*

I WALK on the waste-ground for no good reason
Except that fallen stones and cracks
Bulging with weed suit my mood
Which is gloomy, irascible, selfish, among the split
 timbers
Of somebody's home, and the bleached rags of
 wallpaper.
My trouser-legs pied with water-drops,
I knock a sparkling rain from hemlock-polls,
I crash a puddle up my shin,
Brush a nettle across my hand,
And swear – then sweat from what I said:
Indeed, the sun withdraws as if I stung.

Indeed, she withdrew as if I stung,
And I walk up and down among these canted beams,
  bricks and scraps,
Bitten walls and weed-stuffed gaps
Looking as it would feel now, if I walked back,
Across the carpets of my home, my own home.

## *Ghosts*

THE terrace is said to be haunted.
By whom or what nobody knows; someone
Put away under the vines behind dusty glass
And rusty hinges staining the white-framed door
Like a nosebleed, locked; or a death in the pond
In three feet of water, a courageous breath?
It's haunted anyway, so nobody mends it
And the paving lies loose for the ants to crawl through
Weaving and clutching like animated thorns.
We walk on to it,
Like the bold lovers we are, ten years of marriage,
Tempting the ghosts out with our high spirits,
Footsteps doubled by the silence....

... and start up like ghosts ourselves
Flawed lank and drawn in the greenhouse glass:
She turns from that, and I sit down,
She tosses the dust with the toe of a shoe,
Sits on the pond's parapet and takes a swift look
At her shaking face in the clogged water,
Weeds in her hair; rises quickly and looks at me.
I shrug, and turn my palms out, begin
To feel the damp in my bones as I lever up
And step toward her with my hints of wrinkles,
Crows-feet and shadows. We leave arm in arm
Not a word said. The terrace is haunted,
Like many places with rough mirrors now,
By estrangement, if the daylight's strong.

## *The Gamut*

THE fire gnarls in the grate, or beams
As the wind stretched on the chimney sucks it bright,
Scorches it up;

That pet of a matchflame
Serves me clouds of calm
At my cigarette,
Flips shadows about, whispers
With its tiny sting, wrings
The wood elderly, pricks at my thumb
Before my breath splits and garottes it.
We hang between extremes.

We've thrown open the window after love
To glow over a snowscape in the tense cold,
Have shrivelled icicles in the warm grasp,
Snapped from our eaves,
While ice-winds scorched our cheeks, made us
Weep with the cold,
Flashed and snapped tears from us . . . .

Legged it for shelter in the sleet. . . .

Walked spattered with sun's coils
Buoyed off the water, under a furnace
Hung just at the right heat.

## TED WALKER

### *Breakwaters*

ELMS are bad, sinister trees.
Falling, one leaf too many,
they kill small boys in summer,
tipped over by a crow's foot,
bored with the business of leaves.

An uneasiness attends
dead elms – timber for coffins,
ammunition boxes. And
breakwaters. Bolts open sores
of orange rust in their flanks,

and yet there is loveliness.
Ultimate green of eelgrass
soothes with the comfort of hair
all the tiny agonies
that crawl in hidden places

and sing when the tide is low
and death is not imminent,
scrabbling in an eczema
of pink and white barnacles
and mussels of midnight blue.

Terrifying as altars
by night, black, a sea-Stonehenge.
Filigrees of little wracks
dance on them at high water
in a devil-dance. They change.

Their male look lasts a few tides;
when the reek is washed away
and the stubble is shaven,

on a tall September night
the sea will take his new brides.

In his calm he will lap them,
then batter their waists away,
emphasize their Celtic heads.
And when they are old and raddled,
thin, thin as a Belsen arm,

they will stand bare and skinny
and their stringent, hard old hearts
will disregard his knocking,
Dour, malignant to the core,
they will try to outlive him.

## *The Skate Fishers*

NOW – as at its first shining
Saturn burns slow and alone
to rise on a sudden night
in time for a tide neaping
to an imminent full moon –
they come to their boats and light

their lamps. Propitious the sound
of the suck and the gunwale's
rough rub on the quaywall stone,
the dry deck strewn with dry sand,
no wind fingering it nor swells
to roll one grain away. Then

offshore, no boards creaking, still
amid stillnesses of sea,
the long throb of engines stopped,
they will wait a while until
indigo water and sky
violet have interlocked.

Nine such nights a year only
they have, and some must be missed,
when they may pay a line low
to the grey scabbed skate that lie
among the boulders buttressed
in – nine nights only to pay

a long line down at the mark
that needs such calm to be found
and held. But when the ratchet
clatters and a kittiwake,
disturbed, rises; when, entwined
in weed, line hisses, at that

taut instant the great skate dives
through his black rock canyon
deep, deep, beating his wide wings
on its walls on, on through caves
of no man's knowing. Upon
some arcane ledge, huge, he hangs

pulsing with irritation.
And at each heave of him pumps
the rod above and sideways,
fretting the tightened line on
a jutting shelf till it snaps.
The men, like petrels, restless,

move on across the surface
veined and broken through the stars'
shattered images to shore:
and the skate, with a grimace
of torn lip, spits blood and goes
to do a killing elsewhere.

## *Cuckoo-Pint*

So cold now. I remember
you – bright hedgerow tarts you were,
flagrant in your big red beads,
cheerful, vulgar and brazen.
But then

in a sudden October
when the white night of winter
came, you put aside your gauds
and took vows. Now you open
again,

hooded, cool and sinister.
I know you for what you are
unveiled: loose, secular brides
frustrated with this convent
torment.

## *Easter Poem*

I HAD gone on Easter Day
early and alone to be
beyond insidious bells
(that any other Sunday
I'd not hear) up to the hills
where are winds to blow away

commination. In the frail
first light I saw him, unreal
and sudden through lifting mist,
a fox on a barn door, nailed
like a coloured plaster Christ
in a Spanish shrine, his tail

coiled around his loins. Sideways
his head hung limply, his ears
snagged with burdock, his dry nose
plugged with black blood. For two days
he'd held the orthodox pose.
The endemic English noise

of Easter Sunday morning
was mixed in the mist swirling
and might have moved his stiff head.
Under the hill the ringing
had begun: and the sun rose red
on the stains of his bleeding.

I walked the length of the day's
obsession. At dusk I was
swallowed by the misted barn,
sucked by the peristalsis
of my fear that he had gone,
leaving nails for souvenirs.

But he was there still. I saw
no sign. He hung as before.
Only the wind had risen
to comb the thorns from his fur.
I left my superstition
stretched on the banging barn door.

## *Porpoises*

SOMETIMES in summer the sea
looks infrangible; dull steel
dimpled like a dinner gong.
The metal may be pitted
at the far rim with the hulk
of a forty-foot basker.

A sudden clap-trap of gulls –
and mackerel-magnetized
the sea scribbles lines of force
to attract crazed porpoises
frantic with feeding and rut
close to an inshore bather.

The cow gives suck as she rolls
through her bull's parabola,
dragging her calf over groynes
in his wake of white lather:
and her broad, round head tumbles
to his rhythm. Her thick lips

curl like a negress's lips.
When she dives her flukes lie poised
on the surface an instant
as she breaks another back
among the perfervid shoal
with an automatic snap

of appalling, fluted jaws.
The herd is sleek and wanton,
frenzied, intent as athletes;
paced by herring, hulls of ships,
they never stop, never sleep.
They copulate on the move.

And sometimes, along the shore,
you come across one stranded
like a great, obscene black slug.
Age, exhaustion, impotence,
but no disease can kill them.
They die when they fall behind.

## DAVID WEVILL

### *Spiders*

MUDDLING up the wooden stairs one night, in my socks
Past screens and shuttered bunting-creviced wallboards,
My tongue dry, but a cool wind puffing thinly soft
Up my torn shirt-front, the dust hot-thick in my hair,
I crossed my sister coming that way in her slip –
The steep way down, half-asleep; her chicken-hearted
breathing
And toes antennaed for spiders or bits of fluff
That might jiggle and spill a mouse. I tasted my own
breath
Kekking, milkweed-sour, after the beer –
But not to budge, or her shriek might wake the house –
Who is it? I didn't know her face –
Such full pails for eyes! she might have been glass;
The roman nose, pink lips peeled white over salt
While ten years woke up and started. . . . I thought myself
Back, a loiterer in jeans, hands spittled with oil
From throbbing handlebars. Wind shoulders the porch,
Flickers the close trees. . . . I held back then
And jammed my buttocks hard against black wood,
My back a prickly heat of rusty nails which
Builders'd slapped in, and left, when the lake was young
With all her forests open to the wind, mated conifers
Exploding dry cones. I listened in the dark,
And thought, this wife won't wait to be woken by me,
But go on down, passing me, always on my left –
Wind clacking the picture-frames through our big house –
I wasn't going to wake her. I mightn't have seemed
Her brother, then, but eight legs sprung on her dream,
Something she'd sense far worse than spiders, on the stair,
That could harm her children. Maybe it wasn't just fear,

Or concern, that made me cringe from her.
Two people who cross in the dark walk nearest to ghosts,
Her terror might have stuck its mouth in me,
And sealed her against a love she could not cope with,
Grinning under heavy sheets, with her heartbeat.

## *Separation*

JETTIES suck, suck.
The broken and muddy water grips
Without purpose. The water has
Nowhere else to go, like ships.

Derricks could be of flesh
But seen through, X-rayed to the bone.
A gaunt skyline geometry,
Abstracts jerking out of human

Eyes a like jaggedness.
I imagine I see you borne
Bobbing on the brown water,
Your round eyes grey under the cold horn

Of the fog. And I touch
The river as if skin met skin,
A body identified
But crabbed, gelid, a frayed fraction,

A hermit grip rising out of the mud.
The parcel of sky, crammed, undelivered
Rains. All across the water
Tugs steam like burning dead.

In an instant the flayed river
Hisses up to the jetties
Crawling as if on legs. The ridge
Of that far bank disappears.

The river's itself. Your head
Bending down over the lettered keys
In your factory-loud office, feels
The waters surge back. You close your eyes.

## *The Birth of a Shark*

WHAT had become of the young shark?
It was time for the ocean to move on.
Somehow, sheathed in the warm current
He'd lost his youthful bite, and fell
Shuddering among the feelers of kelp
And dragging weeds. His belly touched sand,
The shark ran aground on his shadow.

Shark-shape, he lay there.
But in the world above
Six white legs dangled, thrashing for the fun of it,
Fifty feet above the newborn shadow.

The shark nosed up to spy them out;
He rose slowly, a long grey feather
Slendering up through the dense air of the sea.
His eyes of bolted glass were fixed
On a roundness of sun and whetted flesh,
Glittering like stars above his small brain –

The shark rose gradually. He was half-grown,
About four feet: strength of a man's thigh
Wrapped in emery, his mouth a watery
Ash of brambles. As he rose
His shadow paled and entered the sand,
Dissolved, in the twinkling shoals of driftsand
Which his thrusting tail spawned.

This was the shark's birth in our world.

His grey parents had left him
Mysteriously and rapidly –
How else is a shark born?
They had bequeathed him the odour of blood,
And a sense half of anguish at being
Perpetually the forerunner of blood:

A desire to sleep in the currents fought
Against the strong enchaining links of hunger,
In shoals, or alone,
Cruising the white haze off Africa,
Bucked Gibraltar, rode into the Atlantic –
Diet of squid, pulps, a few sea-perch.

But what fish-sense the shark had
Died with his shadow. This commonplace
Of kicking legs he had never seen:
He was attracted. High above him
The sunsoaked heads were unaware of the shark –
He was something rising under their minds
You could not have told them about: grey thought
Beneath the fortnight's seaside spell –
A jagged effort to get at something painful.

He knew the path up was direct:
But the young shark was curious.
He dawdled awhile, circling like a bee
Above stems, cutting this new smell
From the water in shapes of fresh razors.
He wasn't even aware he would strike;
That triggered last thrust was beyond his edgy
Power to choose or predict. This
Was carefully to be savoured first, as later
He'd get it, with expertise, and hit fast.

He knew he was alone.
He knew he could only snap off
A foot or a hand at a time –

And without fuss – for sharks and dogs
Do not like to share.
The taste for killing was not even pleasure to him.
And this was new:
This was not sea-flesh, but a kind
Of smoky scent of suntan oil and salt,
Hot blood and wet cloth. When he struck at it
He only grazed his snout,
And skulked away like a pickpocket–

Swerved, paused, turned on his side,
And cocked a round eye up at the dense
Thrashings of frightened spray his climb touched.

And the thrashing commotion moved
Fast as fire away, on the surface of sun.
The shark lay puzzling
In the calm water ten feet down,
As the top of his eye exploded above
Reef and sand, heading for the shallows.
Here was his time of choice –
Twisting, he thought himself round and round
In a slow circling of doubt,
Powerless to be a shark, a spawned insult.

But while he was thinking, the sea ahead of him
Suddenly reddened; and black
Shapes with snouts of blunted knives
Swarmed past him and struck
At the bladder of sunlight, snapping at it.
The shark was blinded –
His vision came to him,
Shred by piece, bone by bone
And fragments of bone. Instinctively
His jaws widened to take these crumbs
Of blood from the bigger, experienced jaws,

Whose aim lay in their twice-his-length
Trust in the body and shadow as one
Mouthful of mastery, speed, and blood –

He learned this, when they came for him;
The young shark found his shadow again.
He learned his place among the weeds.

## *Street Stroller*

STRIDING too slowly to catch up with that glint of sun
Which might have held a Chinaman, a cat, or a butcher's
Work on a missing body, I know
Health comes with facing horror. I find
Dreams flesh me so closely my muscles become poisoned,
My body fitfully weak as the scene of a murder,
A disappearance, or an unknown animal . . .

Struck dead, this city's pavement spits out rain,
Unfamiliar as New York, or Phoenix. My bedsheets
No laundry would accept now, knowing my sleep –
Such unrest has no specific outside itself.
I have created my city in a minute's open hand.
Its eczema spreads, to infect my whole body.

## *The Crèche*

THE crèche of faces, like wintering crocuses, lay mute under their cauls of white wool. I stood at the extreme end of the room, facing the wide fissured mirror, and tried to identify one child that had its fingers twisted to a hard ball in the rough smock of homespun the nuns had sewn him into.

This one, I knew, was not pitted and scarred like the others, but would have slept in a silksoft crib and blue initialled sheets in the now heavily shelled château. The lamps, looking like nuns' wimples, hung over the stark lines of cots, stiff and crisp, starched cotton such as I'd dreamed of, feeling the lice nip deep in my thick socks, touching tenderly the crescent weal on my belly where the rat had clung scrabbling with its claws.

His face, I sensed, would be free of scars and sores, something perhaps crying a little, softly, to itself, that its guardians could not get at now to retrieve. In the glaring silence of the fusty ward I could still, though barely, hear the seventy-fives, and the bigger guns, one-five-fives and naval guns, and the heavy soft flocculent heave of the mortar-bursts. Looking more intently now, I realized there wasn't time, that soon the tanks, the armoured cars, and the Taubes would be circling the village, and an inky smoke would blot up all daylight at the wire-barred windows of the room, making further searches impractical.

So I shouted out my own name; and the long cot lines froze suddenly still, as if the first mortar shell had just now snapped the roof. But nothing moved or spoke, or cried even, and I saw that the nuns had gone away taking their clay jars and crucifixes with them, out of the village. The face I was searching for lay there, among the others, undiscoverable; and sleeping, I imagined, but with its pink shocked mouth open wide on a high silent wailing that followed me, like the sharp tuning-forks of bullets striking the wires, as I stumbled out into the soft April mud, haunted and nameless, as before, belonging nowhere.

## JOHN FULLER

### *White Queen*

WHO has a feeling she will come one day,
No pretty, silly girl, nor beautiful
Like Marlowe's spirit, unapproachable,
But grey, grey, grey from being shut away?

For this is what the poets will not say:
'Helen grew paler and was old, I fear,
(Sixty at Troy's loud fall) and for a year
Was seen by no one, wandering fat and grey.'

In her appearance all will have their say.
Movements of flesh about eternal needs
Promote the spectacle of Helen's deeds
In the mind's eye at least, but in what way?

What figure scampers as this verse begins,
Ashen and wailing, scattering veils and pins?

### *Band Music*

COWS! Cows! With ears like mouths of telephones!
They creak towards him with their heads thrust out,
So baby wauls among the cabbages
Till Betty runs to kiss his quivering pout
And lumping Ernest takes a stick and stones
To drive them off, cursing their ravages.

'Hush, child,' she whispers, rocking. 'There, there
then!
Watch Ernest. Clever Ernest. Nasty cows.'
Inside the cottage from a dusty box

Thumps martial music. Flowers on Betty's blouse
Grow out in lines like cabbages while men
In gold braid blow among the hollyhocks.

## *Mercury*

SCRAPING from the bench
Silver till it becomes
A quivering kidney, black
Under his thin thumbs,

The young apprentice thinks:
'How hot the sun will get!
When earth and rocks like this
Are liquid but not wet,

What will have happened to me,
Who am the only one?'
He weeps, and a dumb wind
Blows in from Asia, un-

-kempt as a messenger;
It slams the door and moans,
And the fingers work faster
At the end of his long bones.

## *Owls*

THE murderous owls off Malo bay
Can lure a sleepless watchman to the sea,
For their deep singing may be heard
Throughout a night of thunder and their red
Eyes take him dancing silently
Down to the choking sea-bed. Far away
His heavy wife sleeps like the dead
Upon the feathers of a bird.

## *Green Fingers*

### I

LAST year's sticks are holding out
For more. Away with them.

The soil aches, tilting over,
Worms waving from windows.

Then seeds: fine as gunpowder,
Horny as toe-nails. A palaver.

You could say that these shoots
Have done it before: frauds.

But at five my daughter is called
To bed. I am not exactly myself.

The garden is creased with buds.
The scent inhabits the glass.

Hands are finished with the
Amazing thing they recognize.

### II

The pond is hideous, a mug of teeth.
Snouts and flex of lilies rot.

Mud moves with halfpenny frogs
The colour of aniseed.

We tilt the buckets out
To catch the snot of newts

And barrows heave the life away
So that the children will not drown.

Man shudders from ungovernable nature,
His greatest deceit.

After a night of unsettled dreams,
The mirror merciless in horror:

Nose. Vulnerable eyes. Growth
Of hair. The whole stirring.

## IAN HAMILTON

### *The Storm*

MILES off, a storm breaks. It ripples to our room.
You look up into the light so it catches one side
Of your face, your tight mouth, your startled eye.
You turn to me and when I call you come
Over and kneel beside me, wanting me to take
Your head between my hands as if it were
A delicate bowl that the storm might break.
You want me to get between you and the brute
thunder.
But settling on your flesh my great hands stir,
Pulse on you and then, wondering how to do it, grip.
The storm rolls through me as your mouth opens.

### *The Recruits*

'NOTHING moves,' you say, and stare across the lawn
At the trees, loafing in queues, their leaves rigid;
At the flowers, edgy, poised. You turn and cry;
'The sun is everywhere. There will be no breeze.'

Birds line the gutters, and from our window
We see cats file across five gardens
To the shade and stand there, tense and sullen,
Watching the sky. You cry again: 'They know'.

The dead flies pile up on the window sill.
You scoop them into heaps. You weep on them.
You shudder as the silence darkens, till
It's perfect night in you. And then you scream.

## *Trucks*

At four, a line of trucks. Their light
Slops in and spreads across the ceiling,
Gleams, and goes. Aching, you turn back
From the wall and your hands reach out
Over me. They are caught
In the last beam and, pale,
They fly there now. You're taking off, you say,
And won't be back.
                    Your shadows soar.
My hands, they can merely touch down
On your shoulders and wait. Very soon
The trucks will be gone. Bitter, you will turn
Back again. We will join our cold hands together.

## *Last Illness*

Entranced, you turn again and over there
It is white also. Rectangular white lawns
For miles, white walls between them. Snow.
You close your eyes. The terrible changes.

White movements in one corner of your room.
Between your hands, the flowers of your quilt
Are stormed. Dark shadows smudge
Their faded, impossible colours
But do not settle.

You hear the ice take hold. Along the street
The yellowed drifts, cleansed by a minute's fall,
Wait to be fouled again. Your final breath
Is in the air, pure white, and moving fast.

## *Pretending not to Sleep*

THE waiting rooms are full of 'characters'
Pretending not to sleep.
Your eyes are open
But you're far away,
At home, *am Rhein*, with mother and the cats.
Your hair grazes my wrist.
My cold hand surprises you.

The porters yawn against the slot-machines
And watch contentedly; they know I've lost.
The last train
Is simmering outside, and overhead
Steam flowers in the station rafters.
Soft flecks of soot begin to settle
On your suddenly outstretched palms.
Your mouth is dry, excited, going home;

The velvet curtains,
Father dead, the road up to the village,
Your hands tightening in the thick fur
Of your mother's Persian, your dreams
Moving through Belgium now, full of your trip.

## INDEX OF FIRST LINES

## INDEX OF POETS

## *Poetry Books in Penguins*

A selection

*James Fenton*
*The Memory of War and Children in Exile*
*Poems 1968–83*

'He is alone among his contemporaries in having a great deal to write *about* ... a vision of recent history, and his own personal place in it ... a view of life that is stylish, wary, provisional, always intelligent, never breast-beating' – Jonathan Raban in the *Sunday Times*

*Octavio Paz*
*Selected Poems*
A bilingual edition, edited by Charles Tomlinson

A dazzling and mercurial writer equally at home with French Surrealism, American poetry, German Romanticism and Marxist polemic, Paz is clearly established as one of Latin America's greatest poets.

*Günter Grass*
*Selected Poems*
Translated by Michael Hamburger
and Christopher Middleton

A bilingual selection of his poetry 'exposing the false identities of modern man, the fragmentation of his world, his puzzlement, his littleness and his curious paradoxical courage in recognizing absurdity and facing it'.

## *Poetry Anthologies in Penguins*

A selection

*The Penguin Book of Greek Verse*
Edited by Constantine A. Trypanis

This selection of Greek Verse in the original is the first of its kind to be published in the English-speaking world: it covers approximately three thousand years – from Homer to the twentieth century.

*The Penguin Book of English Verse*
Edited by John Hayward

A choice of verse reflecting the richness and variety of intellectual and emotional appeal made by the principal poets – some 150 in all – who have written in English throughout the four centuries dividing the first Elizabethan age from the second.

*The Penguin Book of Irish Verse*
Introduced and edited by Brendan Kennelly

Brendan Kennelly explores the origins and development of the Irish poetic tradition, tracing its growth to show its tough capacity for survival despite long silences and methodical oppression and indicating the directions in which he believes it is likely to develop.

## *Poetry Anthologies in Penguins*

A selection

*The Penguin Book of Love Poetry*
Introduced and edited by Jon Stallworthy

Set by theme rather than chronology, Jon Stallworthy's delightful anthology explores men and women's changeless responses to the changeless changing seasons of their hearts.

*A Choice of Comic and Curious Verse*
Edited by J. M. Cohen

This volume covers the whole tradition of English and American comic verse writing from the masters – Hood, Lear, Carroll – to anonymous lampoonists of the eighteenth century, up to the present day.

*The Penguin Book of Ballads*
Edited by Geoffrey Grigson

From both Britain and overseas, this rich and colourful selection of traditional and modern ballads includes stories of court, castle and manor, and themes of social injustice, love and war.

*The Penguin Book of First World War Poetry*
Edited by Jon Silkin

In this haunting collection of war poetry, poets who were soldiers are joined by others like Kipling and Hardy who were not combatants yet wrote poetry concerned with the War.